The Ethics of Risk

Also by Sven Ove Hansson

SETTING THE LIMIT: Occupational Health Standards and the Limits of Science

A TEXTBOOK OF BELIEF DYNAMICS: Theory Change and Database Updating

THE STRUCTURE OF VALUES AND NORMS

The Ethics of Risk

Ethical Analysis in an Uncertain World

Sven Ove Hansson
Royal Institute of Technology, Sweden

palgrave
macmillan

Softcover reprint of the hardcover 1st edition 2013 978-1-13733364-3

First published 2013 by
PALGRAVE MACMILLAN

Palgrave Macmillan in the UK is an imprint of Macmillan Publishers Limited, registered in England, company number 785998, of Houndmills, Basingstoke, Hampshire RG21 6XS.

Palgrave Macmillan in the US is a division of St Martin's Press LLC, 175 Fifth Avenue, New York, NY 10010.

Palgrave Macmillan is the global academic imprint of the above companies and has companies and representatives throughout the world.

Palgrave® and Macmillan® are registered trademarks in the United States, the United Kingdom, Europe and other countries.

ISBN 978-1-349-46231-5 ISBN 978-1-137-33365-0 (eBook)
DOI 10.1057/9781137333650

This book is printed on paper suitable for recycling and made from fully managed and sustained forest sources. Logging, pulping and manufacturing processes are expected to conform to the environmental regulations of the country of origin.

A catalogue record for this book is available from the British Library.

A catalog record for this book is available from the Library of Congress.

Contents

List of Figures vii

Preface viii

Introduction 1

Part I Why Risk Is a Problem for Ethics

1 The Uncertainties We Face 7
- 1.1 Risk 7
- 1.2 Uncertainty 11
- 1.3 Great uncertainty 14
- 1.4 Multi-agent interactions 16
- 1.5 Control 17
- 1.6 Conclusion 20

2 Difficulties for Moral Theories 21
- 2.1 The mixture appraisal problem 22
- 2.2 Utilitarianism 23
- 2.3 Deontological theories 28
- 2.4 Rights-based theories 34
- 2.5 Contract theories 37
- 2.6 Conclusion 42

3 Back to Basics 44
- 3.1 Delimiting consequences 44
- 3.2 Beyond broad consequences 49
- 3.3 Causality in reality 51
- 3.4 The (d)elusiveness of total consequences 54
- 3.5 Conclusion 56

Part II Making Prudent Risk Decisions

4 Reflecting on the Future 61
- 4.1 The foresight argument 62
- 4.2 Specifying the branches 65
- 4.3 The value-base 66
- 4.4 The decision criterion 67
- 4.5 Conclusion 71

5 Thinking in Uncertain Terms 74
5.1 The proper use of expected utility 74
5.2 Uncertainty and moral leeway 80
5.3 Uncertainty about probabilities 83
5.4 Mere possibilities 88
5.5 Conclusion 93

Part III Solving Conflicts of Risk

6 Fair Exchanges of Risk 97
6.1 A defeasible right 97
6.2 Reciprocal risk impositions 101
6.3 Justice and equal influence 104
6.4 Conclusion 109

7 Moral Excuses under Scrutiny 111
7.1 Undetectable effects 112
7.2 Consent 116
7.3 Contributions to self-harm 121
7.4 Conclusion and outlook 125

Notes 127

References 146

Index 165

List of Figures

5.1 The probability distribution of the overall treatment effect of a drug 85
5.2 Distribution curves for three drugs 86
5.3 Distribution curves for two drugs 87

Preface

Uncertainty about the future is a prominent feature of moral problems in real life. How can we know what is morally right to do when we do not know what effects our actions will have? Moral philosophy has surprisingly little guidance to offer here. Perhaps less surprisingly, the disciplines that systematize our approaches to risk and uncertainty, such as decision theory and risk analysis, have very little to say about moral issues.

This book is a report from an ongoing endeavour to extend the scope of moral theory to problems of uncertainty and risk. As I hope the book will show, moral philosophy has the capacity to provide insights and even guidance in such issues, but this cannot be achieved by just applying existing theory. We need to develop new moral theory that deals with uncertainty at its most fundamental level. It is the major purpose of the book to show how this can be done.

This work has benefited from co-operation and discussions with a large number of colleagues and from comments and criticism on numerous seminars, workshops and conferences. Thanks to all of you! Special thanks go to Barbro Fröding, Niklas Möller, Klaus Steigleder, Peter Vallentyne and Paul Weirich for their useful comments on a late draft of the book.

Sven Ove Hansson
Stockholm, June 2013

Introduction

We often have to make decisions despite being uncertain about their effects on future events. This applies to decisions in our personal lives, such as the choice of education, occupation, or partner. It applies equally to social decisions, including those in national and international politics.[1] In fact, risk and uncertainty are such pervasive features of practical decision-making that it is difficult to find a decision in real life from which they are absent.[2]

In spite of this, moral philosophy has paid surprisingly little attention to risk and uncertainty.[3] Moral philosophers have been predominantly concerned with problems that would fit into a deterministic world where the morally relevant properties of human actions are both well-determined and knowable.[4] The deterministic bias has remained in later years, in spite of the advent of new disciplines that have their focus on risk and uncertainty, such as decision theory and risk research.[5]

We can see this deterministic bias not least in the stock of examples that are used in moral philosophy. Moral philosophers do not hesitate to introduce examples that are far remote from the conditions under which we live our lives, such as examples involving teleportation and human reproduction with spores. However, it is a common feature of most examples used in moral philosophy that each option has well-defined consequences: You can be sure that if you shoot one prisoner, then the commander will spare the lives of all the others. You know for certain how many people will be killed if you pull or do not pull the lever of the runaway trolley, etc.[6] This is of course blatantly unrealistic. In real moral quandaries, we are seldom sure about the effects of our actions.

It is in one sense quite understandable that moral philosophy has paid so little attention to risk and uncertainty. Like all academic disciplines, moral philosophy has to make its simplifications and idealizations.[7] There is certainly no lack of difficult moral problems to deal with even if we restrict our attention to a counterfactual, deterministic world. But as will be shown in what follows, this is a weak defence since moral philosophers have included a fair amount of other, practically much less important complications into moral theory. The priorities do not seem to be right.

Another possible defence of this inattention relies on the division of labour between disciplines. It could be argued that the complications following from indeterminism should be taken care of in decision theory rather than in moral philosophy. But this picture is oversimplified, not least since the very act of taking or imposing a risk can have ethical aspects in addition to those that materialize only with the realization of its possible outcomes.[8] Therefore, it is not sufficient to leave risk and uncertainty for decision-theoretical optimization to take place after the completion of a moral analysis that abstracts from risk and uncertainty. In order for moral philosophy to deal adequately with the actual moral problems that we face in our lives, it has to treat risk and uncertainty as objects (or aspects) of direct moral appraisal.[9] This will have the effect of complicating moral analysis, but these are complications stemming from its very subject-matter and are avoidable only at the price of increased distance from actual moral life.

This book aims at showing how considerations of risk and uncertainty should inform our fundamental standpoints in moral philosophy. It consists of three parts. The first of these shows why and how risk is a problem for ethics. It begins with a chapter that introduces the varieties of unforeseeable and uncontrollable situations that moral analysis has to deal with. In the second chapter, the major available moral theories are shown to be incapable of providing reasonable action guidance in such situations. This failure is further analysed in the third and final chapter in this part of the book. An underlying, severely unrealistic conception of causality is shown to contribute heavily to the difficulties that conventional ethical theories have in dealing with situations involving risk or uncertainty.

The rest of the book is devoted to the more constructive task of developing a plausible ethical approach to problems involving risk and uncertainty. Its second part is devoted to situations not involving issues of justice or other potential conflicts of interest between people. In the first of these chapters a thought pattern called hypothetical retrospection is introduced for use in moral deliberation under risk and uncertainty. This is followed by a chapter in which this pattern is employed to develop several useful, more concrete patterns of argumentation.

The final part of the book is devoted to conflicts of interest concerning risks and in particular to risk impositions, i.e. actions by one person or group imposing a risk on some other person or group. The first chapter in this part proposes ethical criteria for determining whether a risk imposition is morally justified. These criteria are based on mutually beneficial exchanges of risk-taking. In the book's final chapter, this is followed by a critical assessment of three common excuses for risk impositions. By exposing the weaknesses of these excuses, the chapter reconfirms the need to subject risk impositions to the rather strict criteria that have been developed in previous chapters.

Part I

Why Risk Is a Problem for Ethics

1
The Uncertainties We Face

Before investigating the moral implications of our ignorance about the future, we need to characterize it and clarify the meanings of the words that we use to describe it. The most common of these is 'risk'.

1.1 Risk

The word 'risk' has several well-established usages.[1] Two major characteristics are common to them all. First, 'risk' denotes something undesirable. The tourist who hopes for a sunny week talks about the 'risk' of rain, but the farmer whose crops are threatened by drought will refer to the 'chance' rather than the 'risk' of precipitation.

Secondly, 'risk' indicates lack of knowledge.[2] If we know for sure that there will be an explosion in a building that has caught fire, then we have no reason to talk about that explosion as a risk. Similarly, if we know that no explosion will take place, then there is no reason either to talk about a risk. We refer to a risk of an explosion only if we do not know whether or not it will take place. More generally speaking, when there is a risk, there must be something that has an unknown outcome. Therefore, to have knowledge about a risk means to know something about what you do not know. This is a difficult type of knowledge to assess and act upon.[3]

Among the several clearly distinguishable meanings of the word 'risk', we will begin with its two major non-quantitative meanings. First, consider the following two examples:

> 'A reactor-meltdown is the most serious risk that affects nuclear energy.'

> 'Lung cancer is one of the major risks that affect smokers.'

In these examples, a risk is an *unwanted event* that may or may not occur.[4] In comparison, consider the following examples:

> 'Hidden cracks in the tubing are one of the major risks in a nuclear power station.'
>
> 'Smoking is the biggest preventable health risk in our society.'

Here, 'risk' denotes the *cause* of an unwanted event that may or may not occur (rather than the unwanted event itself). Although the two non-quantitative meanings of 'risk' are in principle clearly distinguishable, they are seldom kept apart in practice.

We often want to compare risks in terms of how serious they are. For this purpose, it would be sufficient to use a binary relation such as 'is a more serious risk than'. In practice, however, numerical values are used to indicate the size or seriousness of a risk.[5] There are two major ways to do this. First, 'risk' is sometimes identified with the *probability* of an unwanted event that may or may not occur.[6] This usage is exemplified in phrases such as the following:

> 'The risk of a meltdown during this reactor's lifetime is less than one in 10,000.'
>
> 'Smokers run a risk of about 50 per cent of having their lives shortened by a smoking-related disease.'

It is important to note that probability, and hence risk in this sense, always refers to a specified event or type of events. If you know the probability (risk) of power failure, this does not mean that you have a total overview of the possible negative events (risks) associated with the electrical system. There may be other such events, such as fires, electrical accidents, etc., each with their own probabilities (risks).

Many authors (and some committees) have attempted to standardize the meaning of 'risk' as probability, and make this the only accepted meaning of the word.[7] However, this goes against important intuitions that are associated with the word. In particular, the identification of risk with probability has the problematic feature of making risk insensitive to the severity of the undesired outcome. A risk of 1 in 100 to catch a cold is less undesirable than a risk of 1 in 1000 to contract a deadly disease. Arguably, this should be reflected in a numerical measure of risk. In other words, if we want our measure to reflect the severity of the risk, then it has to be outcome-sensitive as well as probability-sensitive.[8] There are many ways to construct a measure that satisfies these two criteria, but only one of them has caught on, namely the expectation value of the severity of the outcome.

Expectation value means probability-weighted value. Hence, if 200 deep-sea divers perform an operation in which the risk of death is 0.001 for each individual, then the expected number of fatalities from this operation is $0.001 \times 200 = 0.2$. Expectation values have the important property of being additive. Suppose that a certain operation is associated with a 0.01 probability of an accident that will kill five persons, and also with a 0.02 probability of another type of accident that will kill one person. Then the total expectation value is $0.01 \times 5 + 0.02 \times 1 = 0.07$ deaths. In similar fashion, the expected number of deaths from a nuclear power plant is equal to the sum of the expectation values of each of the various types of accidents that can occur in the plant.[9] The following is a typical example of the jargon:

> 'The worst reactor-meltdown accident normally considered, which causes 50000 deaths and has a probability of 10^{-8}/reactor-year, contributes only about two per cent of the average health effects of reactor accidents.'[10]

The same author has described this as '[t]he only meaningful way to evaluate the riskiness of a technology'.[11] Another example of this approach is offered by risk assessments of the transportation of nuclear material on roads and rails. In such assessments, the radiological risks associated with normal handling and various types of accidents are quantified, and so are non-radiological risks including fatalities caused by accidents and vehicle exhaust emissions. All this is summed up and then divided by the number of kilometres. This results in a unit risk factor that is expressed as the expected number of fatalities per kilometre.[12] The risk associated with a given shipment is then obtained by multiplying the distance travelled by the unit risk factor. These calculations will provide an estimate of the total number of (statistically expected) deaths.

The use of the term 'risk' to denote expectation values was introduced into mainstream risk research through the influential Reactor Safety Study (WASH-1400, the Rasmussen report) in 1975.[13] Many attempts have been made to establish this usage as the only recognized meaning of the term.[14]

The definition of risk as expected utility differs favourably from the definition of risk as probability in one important respect: It covers an

they are unknown. In one of the most influential textbooks in decision theory, the terms are defined as follows:

> 'We shall say that we are in the realm of decision-making under:
>
> (a) *Certainty* if each action is known to lead invariably to a specific outcome (the words prospect, stimulus, alternative, etc., are also used).
> (b) *Risk* if each action leads to one of a set of possible specific outcomes, each outcome occurring with a known probability. The probabilities are assumed to be known to the decision-maker. For example, an action might lead to this risky outcome: a reward of $10 if a "fair" coin comes up heads and a loss of $5 if it comes up tails. Of course, certainty is a degenerate case of risk where the probabilities are 0 and 1.
> (c) *Uncertainty* if either action or both has as its consequence a set of possible specific outcomes, but where the probabilities of these outcomes are completely unknown or are not even meaningful.'[23]

A few comments are in place about the notion of uncertainty. First, uncertainty differs from 'risk' in not implying undesirability. We can have uncertainty, also in this technical sense, about desirable future events.

Secondly, this technical usage of the terms 'risk' and 'uncertainty' differs distinctly from quotidian usage. In everyday conversations, we would not hesitate to call a danger a risk even though we cannot assign a meaningful probability to it. Furthermore, in non-technical language uncertainty is a state of mind, i.e. something that belongs to the subjective realm. In contrast, 'risk' has a strong objective component.[24] If a person does not know whether or not the grass snake is poisonous, then she is uncertain about its ability to poison her. However, since this species has no poison, there is no risk to be poisoned by it. But all this refers only to everyday usage. In the well-established technical usage, the difference between risk and uncertainty does not refer to the subjective–objective dimension but to the availability of adequate numerical probabilities.

Thirdly, although uncertainty and risk are defined as two mutually exclusive concepts, it is in practice common to use 'uncertainty' in lieu of 'risk or uncertainty'. Then 'uncertainty' is used as a general term for lack of knowledge (whether probabilistic or not), and risk is a special form of uncertainty. Following common practice, the term 'uncertainty' will be used here in this more general sense as well. When necessary, qualifiers such as 'in the broad sense' or 'non-probabilistic' can be applied to distinguish between the two senses of the word.

Uncertainty is ubiquitous. Even in cases when the plausibility of a danger can be meaningfully summarized in a probability estimate, this does not mean that there is no non-probabilistic uncertainty. There may yet remain significant uncertainties about the accuracy of the probability estimate. In fact, only very rarely are probabilities known with certainty. The only clear-cut cases of 'risk' (known probabilities) seem to be idealized textbook cases that refer to devices such as dice or coins that are supposed to be known with certainty to be fair. In real-life situations, even if we act upon a determinate probability estimate, we are not fully certain that this estimate is exactly correct; hence, there is uncertainty. It follows that almost all decisions are made 'under uncertainty'.[25]

If a decision problem is treated as a decision 'under risk', then this does not mean that the decision in question is made under conditions of completely known probabilities. Rather, it means that a choice has been made to simplify the description of this decision problem by treating it as a case of known probabilities.[26] This is often a useful idealization, but even when we use it, it is important to keep in mind the distinction between a probability estimate and a known probability.

In some fields of knowledge we have access to estimates of risks that have been made by highly specialized experts. But even when such estimates are based on the best available evidence, their correctness cannot be taken for granted. We know from historical experience that experts are sometimes mistaken. A rational decision-maker should take into account the possibility that this may happen again. Suppose that a group of experts have studied the possibility that a new microorganism that has been developed for therapeutic purposes will mutate and become virulent. They have concluded that the probability that this will happen is 1 in 100,000,000. For the decision-makers who receive their report, the crucial issue need not be whether a risk of that magnitude should be accepted. Instead, it could be how certain the conclusion is.[27]

Unfortunately, this problem has often been neglected. There is a strong tendency in decision-supporting disciplines to proceed as if reliable probability estimates were available for all possible outcomes. This means that all decisions are treated as if they took place under epistemic conditions analogous to gambling at the roulette table (the tuxedo fallacy).[28] This can be a dangerous thought pattern since it may lead to an illusion of control and to neglect of uncertainties that should have a significant impact on decisions.[29]

Admittedly, there is an influential theory, namely Bayesian decision theory, according to which all statements about the world should have a definite probability assigned to them. According to Bayesianism, non-logical propositions should never be fully believed, but only assigned high probabilities. Hence, epistemic uncertainty is always reduced to probability. The resulting belief system is a complex web of interconnected probability statements.[30]

However, Bayesianism has a crucial drawback: It does not take into account the cognitive limitations of actual human beings. We cannot handle the mass of complexly interconnected probabilities that will emerge when probabilities are assigned to each and every sentence about the world. Of course, we may reflect on how a rational being with unlimited cognitive capabilities should behave, but these are speculations with only limited relevance for actual human beings. A much more constructive approach is to discuss how a rational being with limited cognitive capabilities can make rational use of these capabilities.[31] Non-probabilistic uncertainty is an inescapable condition of human life that ethics has to deal with.

1.3 Great uncertainty

The uncertainty discussed above consists in lack of probabilistic knowledge. Life is full of situations where our lack of knowledge goes even further than that. In addition to known dangers for which we have no probabilities, we also have to deal with the fact that we do not know what dangers we may have ahead of us. Suppose that someone proposes the introduction of a genetically altered species of earthworm that will aerate the soil more efficiently. If introduced in nature, it will ultimately replace the common earthworm. For the sake of argument we may assume that all concrete worries have been neutralized. The new species can be shown not to induce more soil erosion, not to be more susceptible to diseases, etc. Still, it would not be irrational to say: 'Yes, but there may be other negative effects that we have not been able to think of. Therefore, the new species should not be introduced.' Similarly, if someone proposes to eject a chemical substance into the stratosphere in order to mitigate the greenhouse effect, it is not irrational to oppose this proposal solely on the ground that it may have consequences that we have not even been able to think of.[32] Some recent debates on biotechnology and nanotechnology exemplify this type of problem. The focus in these debates has often been on vague or unknown dangers such as the creation of new life-forms with unforeseeable properties.[33]

The type of uncertainty exhibited in these examples can be referred to as *unknown possibilities*. It can in principle be represented in a probabilistic framework as the existence of some consequence for which we do not know whether its probability is zero or non-zero. However, such a probabilistic representation does not capture the gist of the matter. The characteristic feature of these cases is that we do not have a complete list of the consequences that should be taken into account.

It is usually taken for granted in ethical theory (and also in decision theory) that the values on which we base our decisions are well-defined and sufficiently precise. In practice, this is often not the case. One important reason for this is that the alternatives we compare are insufficiently specified for the evaluation. I do not know which I prefer, €8,000 or that my child gets a better mark in math. If I am actually placed in a situation where I can choose between the two, the circumstances will be crucial for my choice. (Is the offer an opportunity to bribe the teacher, or is it an efficient extra course that I only have to pay for if the child achieves a better mark?) I have no general-purpose preference between €8,000 and my child getting a better mark in math, simply because my willingness to pay will depend on the circumstances. In a case like this, we may assume that value comparability can be obtained if the alternatives are sufficiently specified. In other cases, this may not be so. We may be genuinely uncertain about how we would compare for instance a large increase in the prevalence of non-lethal asthma to a much smaller increase in the prevalence of a deadly disease. In some such cases, it is quite plausible that no amount of further specification will resolve the issue. In many social decisions, we have to compare complex outcomes that differ in terms of categories that are very difficult to compare, such as money, human lives, human well-being, preservation of the natural environment, etc.[34]

It is also usually taken for granted in ethics and decision theory that the alternatives we can choose between are well-defined. In actual practice, this is often not the case. Most decisions are parts of larger decision complexes that can be divided into smaller and more manageable decisions in many different ways. The delimitation of the decision is often controversial among those who participate in it or try to influence it. Hence, the nuclear waste issue is addressed by the nuclear industry as a choice between different waste disposal methods. In contrast, many environmentalists tend to see the issue of nuclear waste as an integrated part of the much larger decision whether to deploy nuclear energy in the future. Uncertainties like this can be called *uncertainties of demarcation*.

Great uncertainty is a general term for lack of knowledge that goes beyond lack of probabilities for a well-defined set of outcomes.[35] Great uncertainty includes unknown possibilities, uncertain values, and uncertain demarcation. These different forms of great uncertainty all have in common that they are difficult if not impossible to express in probabilistic terms.

1.4 Multi-agent interactions

You are not alone in making choices and decisions with an impact on the future. Unless you live the life of an eremite, the effects of your actions are combined with those of others, giving rise to compound effects that do not follow from your own actions alone. We all try both to influence the choices that others make and to foresee them and adjust to them. Therefore, our choices will depend in part on how we expect others to react and behave, and conversely their choices will depend on what they expect from us.

Such interactions are extremely difficult to capture in probabilistic terms. This applies in particular to malevolent action, such as the actions of an enemy, a saboteur, or a terrorist. Such agents try to take their adversaries with surprise. It is in practice impossible – and perhaps even counterproductive – to make probability estimates of their future actions. For most purposes, a game-theoretical approach that makes no use of probabilities is more adequate to deal with inimical actions than a decision-theoretical one that uses probability estimates. Security analysts tend to focus on identifying possibilities, e.g. possible routes and goals of malevolent actions, rather than on estimating their probabilities.

Recent experiences have reminded us that the possibility of malevolent action has to be taken into account in many social decisions. We have to ask questions such as: Will the construction of the world's highest building provoke terrorist attacks? Will a politically controversial power transmission system attract attacks by political extremists? How vulnerable is the city's water system to sabotage? These are all issues of security, i.e. protection against intentional threats, in contrast to safety, i.e. protection against unintentional threats. Traditionally, safety and security have been dealt with as separate issues. In many organizations that have to deal with both types of issues, surprisingly little has been done to coordinate them.

For a simple example, suppose that in order to reduce the risk of explosion in a chemical plant we have removed all ignition sources from the vicinity of explosive materials. This can be an efficient way to reduce the probabilities of several types of accidents. However, it is of no use if terrorists arrive to attack the plant. They are sure to bring their own ignition sources. There are other, perhaps more cumbersome measures that will have effects against both accidents and vicious attacks, such as replacing explosive substances by a non-explosive ones, reducing the inventories of explosive and flammable substances, removing the remaining stocks from places where many persons are present, etc.[36]

Cases with malevolent action are particularly clear examples of how multi-agent situations differ from cases with only one agent. However, other types of multi-agent interactions have similar features. If you want to make friends with a person, then your success in doing this will depend on a complex interplay of actions by both of you. The same applies if you want to achieve a desired outcome in a negotiation or if you try to make a vacation trip with a group of friends agreeable to all participants. In these and many other cases, we need to take into account a whole series of interactions that do not seem to be representable in probabilistic terms. When preparing plans for your joint vacation, it does not seem useful to make probability estimates of your companions' reactions to different proposals. It would be more useful to interact with them with the purpose of finding a plan that is agreeable to all of you. If you need any formal support for that activity, then you can expect game-theoretical models to be more helpful than probabilistic ones.

1.5 Control

Both in decision theory and modern ethics, problems are usually presented in the format of a single, 'one-shot' decision, i.e. a situation in which a decision-maker has exactly one decision to make. This approach is inherent in the standard decision-theoretic formalism, namely decision matrices. (In this framework, a series of several decisions can be reduced to a single decision on how to act in all possible future situations.[37]) This is one of the features of decision theory that have had a deep influence on moral philosophy.[38] Problems discussed in modern ethics usually concern how one should make one particular decision, rather than, for instance, how one should lead one's whole life. But in practice we have to make many decisions that are entangled in complex ways. Instead of a single decision point, we have a series of (largely unknown) future decision points ahead of us. How should such future decisions be dealt with when we make the first (or the next) decision in that series?

The crucial issue here is whether or not one should treat one's own future choices and decisions as under one's present control.[39] If we treat them as *not* under our present control, then we have a choice between several alternative approaches, such as assigning probabilities to them, treating them as unprobabilizably uncertain, and treating them game-theoretically. Only one of these options seems to have been dealt with in the literature, namely that of making a probabilistic assessment of how one will act in the future decision situation, just as one might have done for a natural event. Therefore, the problem of control has often, but somewhat misleadingly, been discussed as a choice whether or not to assign probabilities to one's own future actions.

The problem can be described with somewhat more precision as follows: The consequences at time t_3 of your actions at time t_1 are not determinate if you have an intermediate decision point t_2 at which you can influence what happens at t_3. In a moral appraisal of your actions at t_1, you have to decide whether to treat your actions at t_2 as under your own control at t_1 or as beyond your control at that point in time. In the former case, a decision at t_1 can bind your actions at t_2; in the latter case it cannot do so. The following two examples illustrate the problem:[40]

> *Example 1.1*: A non-smoker considers the possibility of smoking for just three weeks and then stopping, in order to achieve a better understanding of why so many people smoke. When making this decision she may regard herself as being in control of her future decision whether or not to stop at the end of the third week. Under this assumption, a trial period of three weeks does not seem unreasonable. Alternatively, she can make a probabilistic appraisal of what she will do in that situation. Under the latter assumption, trying to smoke would seem to come out as a much too dangerous operation.
>
> *Example 1.2*: A heavy cigarette smoker considers whether or not to try to quit. Statistics available to her show that among people in her own age group and socioeconomic group who have smoked as much as she has, almost everyone who tries to quit fails. When making this decision, she may regard herself as being in control of future decisions whether or not to start smoking again. An analysis based on these assumptions will provide her with good reasons to try to stop smoking. Alternatively, she can make a probabilistic appraisal of her future decisions. From such a viewpoint, quitting may seem to have a too meagre prospect of success to be worth trying.

Probably, most of us would prefer the non-control assumption in Example 1.1, and the control assumption in Example 1.2. But other examples can be constructed that are more difficult to decide:

> *Example 1.3*: On New Year's Eve I decided to go to the gym twice a week the following year. The cheapest option is to buy a 12 months gym membership. However, if I fail to carry out my decision and only go to the gym a few times, it will be much cheaper to buy a ticket for each visit. But on the other hand, having paid in advance for the whole year may be a factor that induces me to go to the gym. Should I buy the membership?

My decision in this case will probably depend on a mixture of empirical considerations (how useful is the gym for me, how expensive is the membership, etc.) and moral or prudential considerations (how important is it to foster the virtue of self-control, how blameworthy is it to have unrealistic beliefs about one's own self-mastery, etc.).[41]

No general rule seems to be available to determine whether or not one should act in a specific situation as if one is in control of one's own future actions. Theoretically, we tend to treat this as an all-or-nothing issue: either one has control or one does not. In practical situations, there is often uncertainty about our control over future actions, i.e. we do not know if we will be able or willing in the future to carry through the decisions we make today.

We tend to draw the limits of control wider in cases of success or potential success than in cases of failure. A student who obtained excellent results despite unfavourable circumstances will usually be given credit for her achievement. Many of us are more reluctant to blame a student who failed under comparable circumstances, presumably because we are not sure that the outcome was under her control. Similarly, in a medical context patients are often encouraged to take control over their situation, for instance, by reducing their calorie intake or refraining from alcohol. However, when this fails, the professional attitude is not to blame the patient for the failure but instead to search for new ways to help her.[42]

As these examples show, how much control we ascribe to a person depends not only on the factual circumstances but also on (mostly implicit) ethical considerations. There is always uncertainty about how much control we (now) have over our (future) actions. This factual uncertainty leaves a wide scope for non-factual, in particular ethical, considerations to influence our ascriptions of control. A physician has good ethical reasons to choose different responsibility ascriptions when talking to a patient who contemplates trying to stop smoking and a patient who has failed to do so. In the former case, encouraging the patient to believe in her chances to control her smoking may well help her to achieve her goal. In the latter case, such a belief may instead give rise to self-recrimination that stands in the way of new attempts to solve the problem.

1.6 Conclusion

Both in our private lives and in social decision-making, we encounter uncertainties of widely divergent types. As we have seen, there are cases when the possible outcomes are known and can be assigned meaningful probabilities. But there are also cases when the probability estimates are uncertain, when no meaningful probabilities are available, when we do not have a complete list of the available options, when the behaviour of others cannot be treated probabilistically, when a person's control over her own future actions cannot be determined, etc. These various forms of uncertainty all have implications that need to be taken into account in moral analysis.

The totality of this uncertainty cannot be captured by assigning probabilities to a set of well-determined outcomes. In order to deal adequately with the problems of risk and uncertainty, we must give up the common assumption that all forms of human uncertainty must have the structure of probabilities, i.e. the same structure as the frequencies of events in nature. (In some cases it can even be counterproductive to think in terms of numerical probabilities. In Sweden, about 40 per cent of all marriages end in a divorce.[43] If all spouses in the country based their degree of commitment to the marriage on this probability, then the frequency of divorce might well be still higher.)

We need methods of ethical analysis that can deal with probabilities, but since many types of uncertainty have no credible probabilistic representation, that is not enough. We also need methods of ethical argumentation and analysis that can deal successfully with the other forms of uncertainty that we encounter in real life.

2
Difficulties for Moral Theories

Can moral philosophy deal adequately with risk and uncertainty? Since only a few attempts have been made to apply moral theories systematically to risk and uncertainty, we do not have an extensive catalogue of previous such applications to evaluate. Instead, we will have to investigate the potential capacities of moral theories to solve problems involving risk and uncertainty.

For this investigation we need a uniform format for moral problems that can be used to test different moral theories in a reasonably comparable way. Such a format will be delineated in Section 2.1.

The assessment of a particular (type of) moral theory, such as utilitarianism or some branch of it, will refer here to the use of this theory as the ultimate moral criterion. For instance, when discussing utilitarianism we will focus on moral theories that have a utilitarian rule as their highest principle. Such theories may include deontological concerns, but these concerns are always subservient to a utilitarian final arbitration. Similarly, by a deontological theory will be meant one whose highest principles are deontological. In such a theory, utilitarian concerns may have a place, but they are always subordinate to the overall deontological structure. In other words, a structure of moral thought will be assumed that places one type of moral reasoning above all the others. Such a structure is typical of current moral theory. The structure of everyday moral reasoning is different. There we often combine utilitarian argumentation (weighing pros and cons) with deontological or rights-based argumentation, without assigning to one of them the role of a superior principle to which the others should be subordinated.[1] Such imprecise combinations of moral theories are difficult to evaluate since they leave it open what the recommendation will be when the different moral theories point in different directions. They will not be covered here.

The moral theories to be investigated are the major theories that have been proposed by moral philosophers as means to determine what is right and wrong in individual cases, and thereby guide actions. We will have a close look at utilitarianism (Section 2.2), deontology (Section 2.3), rights-based ethics (Section 2.4), and contract-based ethics (Section 2.5). Virtue ethics will be left out, not because it is less important (it is not!) but because it differs from these other theories in not purporting to provide us with a general recipe for deciding individual cases.[2]

2.1 The mixture appraisal problem

As a car-driver I am not allowed to run over a pedestrian. It is also forbidden for me to drive my vehicle in such a way that there is a probability of 1 in 10 that I run over a pedestrian.[3] However, it is obviously not forbidden to drive in such a way that this probability is 1 in 1,000,000,000 – it would then not be permitted to drive a car at all. In the latter case, the causal connection between the act of driving and the deadly consequence has been drastically diluted. But how much dilution is required to make the action permissible? This is an example of the problem how to appraise, from a moral point of view, mixtures of actions or their properties.[4] Any account of the ethics of risk and uncertainty will have to deal with this problem. It will therefore be used here as a general problem format for assessing how different moral theories can deal with uncertainty. It can be expressed as follows:

> *The mixture appraisal problem (general version):*
> Given the moral appraisals that a moral theory T makes of value-carriers with well-determined properties, what moral appraisals does (a generalized version of) T make of a mixture of such value-carriers?

Four of the terms used in this definition are in need of comments. First, 'moral appraisal' covers a wide range of assignments of moral status, such as declarations that something is forbidden, permitted, morally required, good, bad, better than some specified alternative, etc. In particular, 'moral appraisal' covers both moral norms and moral values – two separable categories that are often inappropriately conflated.[5] Secondly, the term 'value-carrier' covers everything that can be assigned (moral) value, including human actions and their outcomes.[6] The value-carriers to be investigated here are human actions. Thirdly, by a 'mixture' of value-carriers is meant a set of value-carriers such that it is not well-determined which of them will materialize.[7] Finally, the term 'property' is intended to be broadly interpreted. The properties of actions that influence their moral appraisal differ between moral theories. Some but not all of these properties are subsumable under the category of consequences.[8]

A mixture in the intended sense may be either probabilistic or not, depending on whether probabilities have been assigned to its components. This distinction corresponds to that between decision-making under risk and under uncertainty. The probabilistic version of the mixture appraisal problem conforms closely with the framework of risk analysis, in which risks are characterized by the values and probabilities of their possible outcomes.[9] The probabilistic version can be restated as follows:

> *The mixture appraisal problem (probabilistic version):*
> Given the moral appraisals that a moral theory *T* makes of value-carriers with well-determined properties, what moral appraisals does (a generalized version of) *T* make of a probabilistic mixture of such value-carriers?

Our investigation will begin with utilitarianism. This is the moral theory that has the most well-developed strategies for dealing with risk. Although problems of risk and uncertainty have not been much discussed in philosophical utilitarianism, other disciplines such as risk analysis and risk-benefit analysis have developed approaches to risk that have distinctly utilitarian structures.

2.2 Utilitarianism

Amartya Sen provided a useful characterization of utilitarianism as consisting of three main components, namely (1) consequentialism, (2) welfarism, and (3) sum-ranking.[10] By consequentialism is meant that the moral appraisal of an action is completely determined by its consequences. In some versions of utilitarianism, consequences are conceived broadly, so that the consequences of an action can include the infringement of a right or the breach of a prohibition. (We will return in Chapter 3 to the definition and delimitation of consequences.)

Welfarism means that the welfare of individuals is all that matters in the normative assessment of actions, or more precisely that 'a vector of measures of individual well-being, with one element for each relevant individual, exhausts the stock of ethically relevant information in any particular state of the world.'[11] Welfarism has many variants, depending on how well-being is defined.[12] In combination, consequentialism and welfarism imply that if the consequences for individual welfare of an action are known, then enough is known for morally appraising it. Finally, sum-ranking means that an action is assessed according to the sum of a specified set of variables. In combination with the two other components, this means that an action is morally appraised according to the sum of the values of its consequences for individual welfare for all affected individuals.

With these specifications of utilitarianism, the mixture appraisal problem can be rephrased as follows:

> *The mixture appraisal problem for utilitarianism:*
> Given the utilities that a utilitarian theory assigns to (potential) outcomes with well-determined properties, what utilities does (a generalized version of) this theory assign to mixtures of such outcomes?

Two major solutions to this problem are available, namely actualism (actual consequence utilitarianism) and expected utility maximization.[13] The former can be defined as follows:[14]

> *Actualism:*
> The utility of a mixture of potential outcomes is equal to the utility of the outcome that actually materializes.

Actualism has several fairly obvious problems in terms of its applicability. In order to apply it in a moral evaluation of some action that has been performed, we have to compare the actual consequences of that action to the actual consequences of alternative actions that have not been performed. As has been pointed out by Marcus Singer and others, this is an impossible comparison since unrealized alternatives have no actual consequences. Therefore, they cannot be evaluated according to actualist criteria.[15] The standard method to get around this difficulty is to introduce counterfactual consequences. Then the actual consequences of the performed action are measured against the consequences that each of the unperformed actions would have given rise to if it had been performed.[16] However, this is not a comparison on an equal level, since counterfactual consequences are less well-defined than actual consequences. Suppose that after some hesitation I gave my child a dog. There were thousands of ways in which I could have done this (different dogs, different rules about the child's responsibility for the animal, etc.), but for the actualist evaluation only one of them – namely the way in which I actually did it – has to be assessed. There were also a large number of ways in which I could have carried out a decision not to give the child a dog. Since none of these was performed, none of them stands out as the only one that needs to be assessed in an actualist evaluation. This makes the assessment more vague and uncertain than that of the action that was actually performed.

Actualism also has another, equally serious problem: Even for the alternative that materializes, the consequences can only be known after the fact. I could not know the consequences of giving my child a dog before I did so. Obviously, information that can only be obtained after an action has been performed cannot be used for action-guidance. Hence, if we appraise actions according to the actualist recipe, then we have to compare an alternative whose value-relevant properties can only be known after the fact to other alternatives whose value-relevant properties cannot be determined even after the fact.[17]

But for the sake of argument, let us assume that these problems can in some way be solved so that we can make reasonable moral assessments both of the actual consequences of the chosen action and of the counterfactual consequences of its alternatives. Then yet another serious problem remains, as can be seen from the following examples:

> *Example 2.1:*
> An engineer has to decide whether or not to reinforce a bridge before using it for a single, very heavy transport. There is a 50 per cent probability that the bridge will collapse if it is not reinforced. She decides not to reinforce the bridge. Fortunately all goes well; the bridge is not even damaged.
>
> *Example 2.2*
> A person drives drunk in order to bring a friend (who cannot drive) in time to a meeting. Out of sheer luck she does not cause an accident, in spite of driving dangerously.

According to actualism, the engineer who refrained from safety measures did the right thing, and so did the drunken driver. However, a moral actualist would presumably not recommend people to overload bridges or drive inebriated. These examples show that actualism requires that we use moral terms such as 'right' and 'wrong' in a way that differs radically from ordinary usage. If we accept the actualist interpretation of these words, then it will in most cases be impossible to know beforehand what is right or wrong (or permitted, morally required, good, best, etc.) to do.[18] In this way, action-guidance is expelled from moral discourse. However, action-guidance is largely what we need ethics for.[19] Therefore, this is an unusually unhelpful approach. If we follow it, then action-guidance will have to be reintroduced with some other terminology. It is not clear what would be gained in such a linguistic reshuffle.

The most common utilitarian approach to risk is to assimilate into utilitarianism the standard decision-theoretical method for decision-making under risk, namely expected utility maximization. In this variant of utilitarianism, we are required to choose an action with the highest probability-weighted average of the values of the possible outcomes.

> *Expected utility maximization:*
> The utility of a probabilistic mixture of potential outcomes is equal to the probability-weighted average of the utilities of these outcomes.

Since probabilities are used, this decision rule is only applicable to the probabilistic, not the general, version of the mixture appraisal problem. It corresponds, of course, to the second of the two quantitative risk definitions introduced in Section 1.1, and it is the approach taken in probabilistic risk analysis (PRA) and cost-benefit analysis (CBA). In both these disciplines, probability-weighted averages are used to evaluate alternatives. Cost-benefit analysis is in fact the major form of applied utilitarianism.[20]

Several practical problems are connected with the use of expected utility for moral guidance. It is often difficult or even impossible to determine the exact utilities and probabilities that are needed for the analysis.[21] On a more fundamental level, expected utility maximization is normatively problematic in at least two ways.

First, it cannot be taken for granted that the moral impact of a potential outcome is proportionate to its probability. In policy discussions, the avoidance of very large catastrophes, such as a nuclear accident costing thousands of human lives, is often given a higher priority than what is warranted by the statistically expected number of deaths.[22] Expected utility maximization does not have room for such risk-averse or cautious decision-making. This is problematic since risk aversion appears to be a reasonable approach in many situations.[23]

Secondly, expected utility is impersonal in the same sense as utilitarianism in general. (Expected) utilities and disutilities that pertain to different individuals are added up, with no respect being paid to the fact that they refer to different persons. In this way, a disadvantage affecting one person can always be justified by a sufficiently large advantage to some other person.[24]

> *Example 2.3:*[25]
> In an acute situation we have to choose between two ways to repair a serious gas leakage in the machine-room of a chemical factory. One of the options is to send in the repairman immediately. There is only one person at hand who is competent to do the job. He will run a risk of 0.9 to die due to an explosion of the gas immediately after he has performed the necessary technical operations. The other option is to immediately let out gas into the environment. In that case, the repairman will run no particular risk, but each of 10,000 persons in the immediate vicinity of the plant runs a risk of 0.001 to be killed by the toxic effects of the gas.

In this case, in order to maximize expected utility we would have to send in the repairman to die. This is also a fairly safe way to minimize the number of actual deaths. However, it is far from obvious that it is the only reasonable response to this moral quandary. In this and many other cases, a rational decision-maker may refrain from maximizing expected utility (minimizing expected damage) for a moral reason, namely in order to avoid being unfair to a single individual.

Disregard for distributive concerns is problematic already in standard utilitarianism that only deals with determinate outcomes. When probabilistic mixtures are introduced, an additional way to divide advantages and disadvantages among persons (namely as probabilistic fractions) is made available. This introduces additional ways for utilitarianism to justify disadvantages to some persons by advantages to other persons. In this way, the problems created by utilitarianism's disregard for distributive issues are further aggravated.

In conclusion, we have investigated the two major candidates for a method to extend utilitarianism to a non-deterministic setting, namely actualism and expected utility maximization. Neither of these provides us with plausible action-guidance. No other credible solution to the utilitarian mixture appraisal problem seems to be available.[26] However, although this is a serious problem for utilitarianism, its basic underlying thought pattern – that of weighing advantages against disadvantages – is not a forlorn idea. The difficulties arise when this thought pattern is given the role of a surmounting principle to which all other moral considerations, such as fairness to individuals, should be subordinated. It may still be useful if given a more limited role.

Classical utilitarianism has often been criticized for being unfair to those who are worst off. This feature is mended in prioritarianism, a variant of utilitarianism in which benefits to those who are worse off are given higher weight than benefits to those who are better off.[27] Prioritarianism can be combined with probability-weighing of uncertain outcomes to form a prioritarian expected utility theory.[28] In some cases such a theory will yield more plausible results than standard (utilitarian) expected utility. For instance, suppose that it is allowable for a certain well-off person to expose himself to a danger in order to achieve an advantage for himself. According to the classical theory he is then also allowed to expose a destitute person to the same danger in order to achieve the same advantage for himself. The prioritarian theory disallows this since it gives higher weight to welfare changes affecting the worse-off person. However, in dealings between equally well-off persons the prioritarian version of expected utility does not differ from the standard utilitarian one. According to both theories, if it is allowable for a person to expose himself to a danger in order to achieve an advantage for himself, then he is also allowed to expose some other, equally well-off person to the same danger in order to achieve the same advantage for himself. In order to account for how acceptability or nonacceptability of risk exposure can be bound to distinct persons, a more radical departure from utilitarianism is needed.

2.3 Deontological theories

A deontological (duty-based) ethical theory is one that uses duties (obligations) as its primary moral category.[29] In such a theory, the moral status of an action depends on its conformity to a set of moral obligations. These obligations are not restricted to (but they may include) a duty to produce morally good outcomes. (As usual, obligations and prohibitions will be taken to be interchangeable.[30] An action is prohibited if and only if it is obligatory not to perform it.)

We can distinguish between two types of deontological theories, viz. those employing absolute obligations and those employing defeasible (pro tanto) obligations. Absolute obligations are strongly associated with Immanuel Kant, defeasible obligations with W.D. Ross. Following what I said in the preamble of the present chapter, the focus will be on theories whose ultimate moral criterion is deontological. This excludes

Ross's theory and other theories with defeasible duties, since such theories need a mechanism for choosing among conflicting duties, and that mechanism will have a superior role in relation to the duties.

The mixture appraisal problem for deontological theories can be expressed as follows:

> *The mixture appraisal problem for deontological moral theories:*
> Given the duties that a deontological moral theory assigns concerning actions with well-determined properties, what duties does (a generalized version of) this theory assign concerning mixtures of such actions?[31]

The most obvious extension of a deontological theory to indeterminate cases consists in prescribing that a prohibition to bring about a certain outcome implies a prohibition to bring about an increase in its probability, even if that increase is very small.

> *Probabilistic absolutism for deontological theories:*
> If it is morally prohibited to perform a certain action, then this prohibition extends to all mixtures in which the action has non-zero probability.

Probabilistic absolutism is highly implausible. To see this, consider a system of absolute duties that contains a prohibition to kill other persons. According to probabilistic absolutism, this would imply a prohibition to perform any kind of action that increases the probability that another person will be killed. However, although my duty not to kill you is accompanied by a prohibition against many types of acts that would increase your risk of death, it cannot in practice be accompanied by a prohibition of all such acts. Such a strict interpretation would make human society impossible. As already mentioned, I am allowed to drive a car in the town where you live, although this increases the risk of being killed by me. There are numerous other activities that we are allowed to perform although they imply some (small) increase in the risks that others are exposed to: leaving one's home when a family member has a cold (which increases the probability of transmitting the disease to others), serving one's guests fat or otherwise unhealthy food, heating one's house with a furnace that produces a small amount of dangerous emissions, etc. Probabilistic absolutism would prohibit all such acts, thereby making social life impossible.[32]

In order to solve this problem and make deontology socially viable, duties have to be so constructed that they are applicable in the high-probability but not in the low-probability cases. The most straightforward way to achieve this is to introduce probability limits.

> *Probability limits for deontological theories:*
> Each prohibition of an action is associated with a probability limit. The prohibition extends to a mixture that contains the action if and only if the action has, in that mixture, a probability that is above its probability limit.

The prohibition of homicide could then be associated, for instance, with a probability limit of 0.000,001. Then an action is forbidden by this rule if the probability that it leads to the death of another person is above 0.000,001, otherwise not. But this construction is not credible since it draws the line between acceptable and unacceptable risk impositions with no regard to the benefits associated with the risks under consideration. Most of us would accept a very small probability (say, 0.000,001) of a deadly outcome if it comes from a vaccination against a serious disease, but not if it is caused by a food additive that improves the colour of orange juice. This difference can easily be accounted for in (broadly) deontological terms. Vaccinations are justified by another duty, namely the duty to prevent serious, preventable diseases. There does not seem to be any duty to adjust the colour of orange juice. In order to make room for considerations like this, the binary approach of probability limits would have to be replaced by a mechanism that assigns weights to duties, with decreasing weights as probabilities decrease. Then a slight probability of inflicting a serious disease on a person can be allowed in the vaccination case but not in the food additive case, due to the weight of the contravening duty. In this way, however, we have moved away from theories with a deontological final principle to a form of extended utilitarianism, in which the violation of an obligation has a negative value to be weighed against other values in a procedure that has the structure of a utilitarian calculation.[33]

This problem for the probability limit approach exhibits a general problem for deontological theories: If conflicting obligations are allowed into the system, then some mechanism that goes beyond the postulation of duties is required to adjudicate between them. Since we are investigating moral theories whose highest principles are duties, and since we also require that moral theories be action-guiding, this leads us to attempt the construction of a deontological system whose obligations do not run into conflict:

> *Conflict-free specification for deontological theories:*
> The prohibitions of actions and mixtures of actions that a deontological theory gives rise to have to be so specified that conflicts among them do not arise.

In order to clarify the meaning of this principle, we need to pay some attention to the structure of moral obligations. To begin with, it is important to distinguish between rules of obligation and obligation assessments.[34] An obligation assessment says what is obligatory in the actual state of the world (or any other state of the world that is referred to). It has nothing to say about what obligations obtain in other states of the world. In contrast, a rule of obligation expresses some obligation that holds either in all states of the world or (more commonly) in all states of the world that satisfy certain conditions. When seeing a child beating a cat it would be natural to say: 'You must stop beating the cat. You must not be cruel to animals.' The first of these sentences expresses an obligation assessment and the second a rule of obligation.

A rule of obligation consists of two components: a condition of applicability and a stipulation that is triggered if that condition is satisfied. Consider for instance an anti-bribery rule that disallows judges to accept gifts from litigants. Whenever the condition of applicability is satisfied, i.e. a litigant offers her judge a gift, the stipulation is activated and puts the judge under an obligation not to accept the gift in question.

If someone is obligated to perform two actions that cannot both be performed, then there is a conflict of obligations.[35] Such conflicts are seldom if ever inherent in the moral code (the set of rules of obligation). Instead they arise when the code is applied under specific empirical circumstances. In other words, it would be unusual for a moral code to contain two directly conflicting obligations such as 'You should eat no meat' and 'You should eat at least 300 g of beef each week.' Instead conflicts arise when the conditions of applicability of two obligations with (potentially) conflicting stipulations are both instantiated. For an example, consider the moral code of Anselm, a pious royalist. This code contains the two rules of obligation 'Always bow to the ground when you meet the King' and 'When you are in a sanctuary, pay all your reverence to God and bow to no mortal being.' Anselm obeyed these two rules all his life until one day something unusual happened: When he was standing in front of the cathedral's high altar, the King unexpectedly arrived beside him. It was then impossible for him to comply with both of these obligations.

Anselm's moral code does not satisfy Conflict-free specification. However, it can be made to do so by adjusting the condition of applicability of one of the two rules. The first rule can be revised to 'Always bow to the ground when you meet the King on unsanctified ground.' Alternatively the second can be changed to: 'When you are in a sanctuary, pay all your reverence to God and bow to no other mortal being than the King.' But this is not enough. In order to ensure that these two rules are never involved in a conflict of obligations, additional exception clauses are needed. Surely, Anselm should not pay reverence to the King if the latter travels incognito and an act of obeisance could reveal his identity to potential assassins. Presumably, he should bow to a mortal being in a sacrarium if this is for some strange reason what it takes to dissuade a villain from committing some atrocity. There may also be other exceptions to provide for. In order to comply with Conflict-free specification, these seemingly simple rules of obligation will have to be provided with fairly extensive exception clauses.

This example is by no means unusual. The need for exception clauses arises for almost any rule of obligation that we may think of. As was noted by Frankena, it would be 'very difficult to find a concrete rule which one would insist could never be rightly broken'.[36] Even a strict rule such as one prohibiting homicide would require clauses of exception for extreme cases such as self-defence. The need for exception clauses is even greater for 'weak' rules such as obligations to be polite and to obey minor traffic rules. Each such rule would have to contain exception clauses covering all the situations in which stronger rules in the system would invalidate it. There could be no rule about stopping at red lights that did not contain stipulations about various emergencies such as the prevention of traffic accidents, the transportation of severely ill persons to the hospital, etc.[37] Due to the unpredictability of human life, it is impossible to foresee all the types of situations that can justify exceptions to a rule of obligation. Therefore Conflict-free specification is impossible to apply in practice.

There is one option left that needs to be dealt with: Perhaps it is wrong to put the entire burden of conflict-avoidance on the moral code. Perhaps part of it can instead be borne by the agents. We can often avoid situations in which conflicts between obligations may arise. If Anselm never enters the sacrarium of a church, or at least does so only when he knows that the King is not in the vicinity, then the two rules of obligation will never run into conflict. This approach to conflict-avoidance has been promoted by some moral philosophers. Ruth Barcan Marcus proposed as a second-order regulative principle that we should conduct our lives in ways that minimize the occurrence of moral conflict. 'One ought to act in such a way that, if one ought to do x and one ought to do y, then one can do both x and y.'[38] With this approach, Conflict-free specification can be weakened to the following condition:

> *Conflict evadability for deontological theories:*
> The prohibitions of actions and mixtures of actions that a deontological theory gives rise to have to be so specified that by behaving morally and judiciously, an individual can avoid conflicts among them.

The combination of Conflict evadability and judicious individual behaviour would probably be sufficient to avoid conflicts of obligation such as the following:

> *Example 2.4:*
> Angela has promised Brian to meet him at 4:00 p.m. at the University Library. She has also promised Carol to meet her at 4:00 p.m. at the railway station, thirty kilometres away.

Not much can be said against the recommendation to avoid this type of dilemma-creating behaviour. However, this does not seem to be the way in which most conflicts of obligation arise in practice. The following example appears to be much more typical:

> *Example 2.5:*
> Angela has promised Brian to meet him at 4:00 p.m. at the University Library. She has also promised Carol to meet her at the railway station thirty kilometres away 'at whatever time you arrive. Just send a message.' At 3:30 she receives a message telling her that Carol will arrive at the railway station in about half an hour.

In this case, Angela's promises did not (directly) create a conflict of obligations, but they created a *risk* of a future such conflict. She might have avoided this by making the appropriate reservations, for instance by saying to Brian: 'I will meet you there unless something more important comes up that prevents me from coming.' But generally speaking, our commitments can run into conflict in multitudinous ways that we are unable to foresee and make reservations for. Due to the uncertainty that prevails in our lives, we cannot keep account of all possible future events that may create conflicts among our obligations. Almost any additional commitment increases the risk of a future moral conflict. In order to avoid conflicts as far as possible, we would have to systematically avoid commitments to other people. But such non-committance seems to be a much too high price to pay to avoid conflicting obligations. A human society can only flourish if its members willingly assume social roles and responsibilities that are rich in commitments. Therefore, Marcus's principle of Conflict avoidance is not commendable, and for the same reason the principle of Conflict evadability does not solve the mixture appraisal problem.[39]

In summary, no solution seems to be available for the mixture appraisal problem for deontological theories. Again, it must be emphasized that all this is an argumentation against moral theories that have deontology as their ruling principle. It is not an argumentation against the inclusion of duty-based considerations in moral theories with another structure.

2.4 Rights-based theories

A moral theory is rights-based if it uses rights as its primary moral category, in terms of which recommendations for action are derived. Historically, the most important rights-based theories are natural rights theories and various forms of libertarianism. Can a rights-based theory deal adequately with the mixture appraisal problem?

It could possibly be argued that this section is unnecessary, since rights are just another way to express obligations. If that is the case, then we have already dealt with rights implicitly in the previous section. Indeed, many rights have a correlative obligation. You have a right that I do not puncture your bicycle tyres. I have an obligation not to puncture your bicycle tyres. The right and the obligation express the same moral relationship, only seen from the perspectives of different persons.

However, although many rights have a correlative obligation, this is not true of all of them. There are at least two types of rights that do not involve an obligation.[40] One of these is the categorical permissions, permissions that hold without any triggering performative action. For instance, Aunt Edna may, if she so wishes, bequeath everything that she owns to the Cat Lovers' Animal Welfare Society. This is a right that she has, but it does not involve any obligation.[41] The other category consists of the grantable permissions. These are permissions that obtain (only) if someone performs a symbolic action of permitting (granting permission). As an example, I can allow my neighbour to use my lawn-mower. The option of granting that permission is a right that I have, but it does not involve any obligation.[42]

Since there are rights that do not involve any obligation, rights-based moral theories do not have to be obligation-based (deontological), and therefore they need separate treatment. A further reason for treating them separately is that there are traditions in rights-based ethics that differ from those of classical deontology.

In parallel with deontological theories, we can distinguish between two types of rights-based theories, namely those employing absolute and defeasible rights respectively. An absolute right does not yield to anything else. A defeasible right is only prima facie, and may have to yield to other, weightier moral considerations. To be complete, a theory of defeasible rights will also have to include superior mechanisms for determining when a right should be upheld in spite of some conflicting considerations and when it should not. In line with what I said in the preamble of this chapter, the focus will be on theories whose ultimate criterion is rights-based, i.e. theories of absolute rights.

The mixture appraisal problem for rights-based theories was formulated (in its probabilistic version) by Robert Nozick: 'Imposing how slight a probability of a harm that violates someone's rights also violates his rights?'[43] In somewhat more general language we can restate it, as follows:

> *The mixture appraisal problem for rights-based moral theories:*
> Given the rights that a rights-based moral theory assigns concerning actions with well-determined properties, what rights does (a generalized version of) this theory assign concerning mixtures of such actions?[44]

Just as for deontological theories, one obvious attempt at a solution would be a strict extension from deterministic to indeterministic cases. It could be claimed that if I have a right that you do not bring about a certain outcome, then I also have a right that you do not perform any action that has a non-zero probability of leading to that outcome.

> *Probabilistic absolutism for rights-based theories:*
> If someone has a moral right that a certain action not be performed, then this right extends to all mixtures in which this action has non-zero probability.[45]

Unfortunately, such a strict extension of rights is just as socially untenable as the corresponding extension of duties that was discussed in the previous section. You have a right not to be killed by me, but you do not have a right that I refrain from all actions that would involve an increased risk of you dying, such as driving a car in the town where you live. Such a strict interpretation would make human society just as impossible as the corresponding deontological principle.[46]

The approach with a probability limit can also be applied to rights:

> *Probability limit for rights-based theories:*
> Each moral right that a certain action not be performed is associated with a probability limit. The right extends to a mixture that contains the action if and only if the action has, in that mixture, a probability that is above the probability limit.

However, as Nozick observed, such a solution is not credible since probability limits 'cannot be utilized by a tradition which holds that stealing a penny or a pin or anything from someone violates his rights. That tradition does *not* select a threshold measure of harm as a lower limit, in the case of harms certain to occur.'[47] Admittedly, a moral theory need not treat a slight probability of a sizable harm in the same way that it treats a slight harm. The analogy is nevertheless relevant. The same basic property of traditional rights theories, namely the uncompromising way in which they protect against disadvantages for one person inflicted by another, prevents them from drawing a principled line either between harms or between probabilities in terms of their acceptability or negligibility. More importantly, probability limits would draw the line between acceptable and unacceptable probabilities of harm with no regard to the benefits involved. This is implausible for the same reason as the corresponding deontological principle. In order to avoid this problem we would have to replace the binary approach of a probability limit by some adjudication principle that is sensitive to the relative size of harms and benefits. However, just as for deontological theories, this would lead us to some form of extended utilitarianism, in which the infringement of a right has a negative value that is weighed against other such infringements in some type of calculation.

It remains to investigate – again in parallel with deontology – systems of rights in which conflicts cannot arise or, alternatively, they can be avoided by agents who choose to do so. The first option is expressed in the following principle:

> *Conflict-free specification for rights-based theories:*
> The rights conferred by a rights-based theory have to be so specified that the combined realization of these rights does not give rise to any conflicts.

Unfortunately, Conflict-free specification is equally difficult to satisfy as the corresponding principle for obligations. Many obligations have correlative rights. Therefore, cases of conflicts among rights can easily be obtained through redescription of cases of conflicting obligations. An insolvent who has two creditors but can only pay one of them experiences a conflict of obligations; this is also a conflict between the rights of the two creditors to receive their money. Since bankruptcy can be caused by unforeseeable misfortune, it would be difficult if not impossible to prevent such conflicts of rights from occurring. There are numerous other ways in which two rights can run into conflict due to empirical circumstances.

Next, we can weaken Conflict-free specification, and only require that conflicts of rights be avoidable, rather than impossible:

> *Conflict evadability for rights-based theories:*
> The rights conferred by a rights-based theory have to be so specified that by behaving morally and judiciously, an individual can avoid being involved in conflicts among these rights.

Conflict evadability is subject to the same problems as the corresponding principle for obligations. Rights are largely created by the commitments that we make to each other. Due to the uncertainties under which we live, we have no chance of predicting all the ways in which future developments may create conflicts between the rights that we have contributed to establishing. Therefore, Conflict evadability is as unpromising for rights-based ethics as it is for deontology.

In conclusion, moral theories based on absolute rights do not have the means to deal adequately with the mixture appraisal problem.[48] Again it must be emphasized that this deficiency of a 'pure' rights-based theory does not in any way exclude the use of rights in a moral account of risk. What it speaks against, though, is a model based exclusively on rights as superior principles to which all other principles are subordinate.

2.5 Contract theories

Contract theories have a long history in political and moral philosophy. The idea that human society arose out of a contract among individuals living in a pre-political natural state has roots in antiquity. Originally it was used primarily to question or justify the legitimacy of political authority.[49] This usage was extended by John Rawls who employed contract theory to determine what social and political arrangements are defensible. Since Hobbes, contract theory has also been used as a basis for moral theory. Contract-based moral theory (sometimes called contractualism), derives morality as the mutually advantageous behaviour or rules for behaviour that self-interested individuals would agree to.[50]

The mixture appraisal problem for contract theories can be specified as follows:

> *The mixture appraisal problem for contract theories:*
> Given that a contract-based moral theory prohibits a certain action, under what circumstances does this prohibition extend to a mixture containing that action?[51]

As an example, we expect a social contract to prohibit actions that lead to the death of another person. Under what conditions should it also prohibit actions with a low but non-zero probability of leading to the death of another person? The most obvious solution to this problem is to extend the criterion that contract theory offers for the determinate case, namely consent among all those involved, to cases involving risk and uncertainty. Since consent, as conceived in contract theories, can be either actual or hypothetical, there are two variants of this rule. Let us begin with actual consent:

> *Actual consent:*
> Any mixture with a non-zero probability of giving rise to negative value is allowed if and only if it is accepted by everyone who is affected by this negative value.

In some older versions of contract theory, actual consent was conceived as consent in a historical contract that continues to bind subsequent generations, including ourselves. This approach is particularly implausible for problems involving risk and uncertainty, since the partners of the historical contract could not have known much about risks in modern societies. An even remotely plausible theory of actual consent will therefore have to refer to consent by those actually affected, not by their ancestors.

If consent by all those concerned is required, then each of them has veto power.[52] Important decisions concerning social risks have thousands and sometimes millions of affected persons. With such large numbers of veto carrying persons, chances would be small to make any decision at all. Such a system would be constantly deadlocked and incapable of moving forward. In practice, to avoid such impasses we replace individual consent by consent by a majority. In doing this, however, we leave the grounds of contract theory for the simple reason that a contract is by definition a 'mutual agreement between two or more parties.'[53] It does not bind those who choose not to agree.[54]

In summary, the criterion of actual consent does not provide a reasonable solution to the mixture appraisal problem. We are left then with hypothetical consent:

> *Hypothetical consent:*
> Any mixture with a non-zero probability of giving rise to negative value is allowed if and only if it would be accepted in an ideal decision situation by everyone who is affected by this negative value.

For the rule of hypothetical consent to solve the mixture appraisal problem, the following two conditions have to be satisfied:

(i) The ideal decision situation referred to in the rule must be such that the consensus reached in that situation is binding for real life.
(ii) It should be easier to achieve consensus in the ideal situation than in real life.

No ideal decision situation seems to have been constructed that satisfies both of these criteria. Beginning with (i), proponents of hypothetical contract theory have had difficulties in showing how a contract that has not been made can still have binding force.[55] This is a general problem that applies to deterministic as well as non-deterministic decision situations. With respect to (ii), a problem arises that is specific to risk and uncertainty: None of the ideal decision situations constructed for contract theory seems to make the moral appraisal of risk and uncertainty easier or less dependent on controversial values than the corresponding appraisals in the real world.[56]

True, Rawls's initial situation differs from most constructions used in moral theory in containing an essential component of uncertainty. The participants in his original position, the hypothetical gathering at which the fundamental agreement is reached, are placed behind a veil of ignorance:

> 'First of all, no one knows his place in society, his class position or social status; nor does he know his fortune in the distribution of natural assets and abilities, his intelligence and strength, and the like. Nor, again, does anyone know his conception of the good, the particulars of his rational plan of life, or even the special features of his psychology such as his aversion to risk or liability to optimism or pessimism. More than this, I assume that the parties do not know the particular circumstances of their own society. That is, they do not know its economic or political situation, or the level of civilization and culture it has been able to achieve. The persons in the original position have no information as to which generation they belong.'[57]

On the other hand, the participants are supposed to know the effects of all possible choices of a social system; in particular they have to know the effects of various economic arrangements on the social conditions of the least advantaged representative person.[58] (Note that since the participants are assumed to be ignorant of their degrees of aversion to risk their comparisons of different economic systems have to be invariant under changes in the degree of risk aversion.) Therefore, the uncertainty that prevails in Rawls's initial situation is not the uncertainty in the real world that we discussed in Chapter 1. Instead, it is hypothetical uncertainty about some of the things that we are certain of in real life. The initial situation introduces a strange combination of ignorance about that which we in fact know and knowledge about that which we in fact do not know.[59]

Can the Rawlsian approach to uncertainty be extended so that it also covers the uncertainties of the real world? In other words, can we solve the mixture appraisal problem by introducing real-world uncertainty into the initial situation and deal with it in the same way as the artificially introduced (Rawlsian) uncertainty for which the initial situation was constructed?

Unfortunately, this does not seem to be possible. Rawls's approach to hypothetical uncertainty breaks down when ordinary real-life uncertainty is introduced into it. That is because his solution is based on the maximin decision rule. According to that rule, we have to identify, for each alternative action, its security level, i.e. (the value of) the worst possible outcome that it can give rise to. We are then required to choose an alternative with a maximal security level, thus maximizing the minimal outcome. When applied to the original Rawlsian problem this rule selects the social system that is best for the worst-off (representative) members of society. When applied to actual risk-taking, it requires that we completely disregard all but the worst possible outcomes of an action. Such a decision rule will yield highly implausible results.

> *Example 2.6:*
> A physician has to decide whether or not to offer a patient potentially life-saving surgery. If the surgery is not performed, then the patient is sure to die from her disease in between three and twelve months. With surgery, the most probable outcome is complete recovery. However, there is also a significant risk with a probability of about 1 per cent that she will die on the operating table.

Under the assumption that immediate death is the worst outcome, the maximin rule will lead to a decision not to offer the operation. This is a strange recommendation that speaks against the use of the maximin rule.

The maximin rule also has another serious problem: It is extremely sensitive to how we choose to describe or delimit a moral decision. We normally exclude from consideration a large number of possible outcomes that are associated with implausible states of nature. The exclusion of outcomes with very low probabilities usually has negligible impact on decisions made according to expected utility maximization or some other probability-sensitive decision rule. In contrast, the inclusion or exclusion of low-probability outcomes will often be the decisive factor that determines a decision according to the maximin rule. The reason for this is that the latter rule attends exclusively to worst cases, irrespective of how improbable they are. In practice, this means that although the maximin rule is precise enough when applied to an already stated decision problem, it does not help us very much in dealing with an informal problem that has not yet been delimited. The difficulties are only transferred from the analysis to the prior construction of a formal decision problem, in particular to the choice whether to include or exclude various improbable negative outcomes.

One possible response to these difficulties is of course that when real-world decision problems are inserted into Rawls's initial situation, then some other decision rule than the maximin rule should be used. The use of some other rule than maximin in the initial situation is not a strange idea. Indeed, Harsanyi proposed the application of expected utility maximization to solve the problem for which Rawls uses the maximin rule, namely the choice of appropriate social and political arrangements.[60] However, if we are going to apply expected utility maximization to the mixture appraisal problem, then there is nothing to be gained by inserting the mixtures into a hypothetical contract situation. Such a procedure would not make use of the specific resources of the initial situation, and it would not be a contract-based solution in any interesting sense.

In summary, neither an actual nor a hypothetical version of contract theory seems to offer a solution to the mixture appraisal problem. Again, it must be emphasized that this is not an argument against the use of (actual or hypothetical) agreements as elements of a moral theory. It is an argument against their use as a superior principle that defeats all other moral considerations.[61]

2.6 Conclusion

We have investigated four major types of moral theories in order to determine whether they are capable of providing plausible action-guidance for the mixture appraisal problem. The four types are those whose ultimate criterion is utilitarian, deontological, rights-based, and contract-based, respectively. None of these types of moral theories was found capable of dealing satisfactorily with the mixture appraisal problem. This is only one of the several types of uncertainty-related problems that a moral theory should be capable of dealing with, but failure to deal satisfactorily with one such problem is sufficient to show that a moral theory does not have the capacity to solve uncertainty-related problems in general.

For each of the four types of moral theories, we have identified deficiencies that come out when they are applied to ethical problems involving risk and uncertainty. Beginning with utilitarianism, it is deeply affected by two simple facts about consequences: First, the consequences of the actions we perform cannot be determined beforehand. Secondly, the consequences of the alternative actions that we do not perform are not well-defined even after the fact. In combination, these two difficulties prevent actualist versions of utilitarianism from making any progress. The expected utility version of utilitarianism has other problems. Already in its deterministic variant, utilitarianism exhibits a problematic disregard for persons. This becomes even more damaging when probabilistic mixtures are introduced and evaluated with the expected utility rule. These mixtures provide additional ways to divide advantages and disadvantages between persons. They thereby provide additional means to justify disadvantages to one person by the sum of advantages to other persons. Utilitarianism has no barrier against exposing some persons to risk in order to obtain advantages for other persons. A plausible account of the ethics of risk-taking should include barriers against such arrangements.

In deontological and rights-based theories, other problems come out. First, the absolutism of these theories breaks down when they are applied to actions with low probabilities of some undesirable outcome. Neither deontological nor rights-based ethics contains resources of its own to adjust the assessment of a risk to the benefits that are associated with it. Secondly, the prevalent uncertainty in our lives makes it impossible to avoid situations that lead to conflicts between obligations or rights. Since we cannot foresee how future events can create such conflicts, we cannot prevent them from occurring either. Neither deontological nor rights-based theories contain internal resources to resolve these unavoidable conflicts.

Contract theory employs either actual or hypothetical consent as its ultimate moral criterion. In complex issues of risk that involve many persons, a requirement of actual consent would almost unavoidably lead to stalemates. Therefore, actual consent is not workable. Hypothetical consent has other problems as we saw when considering its most well-developed framework, the Rawlsian initial situation. It was constructed to deal with hypothetical uncertainties such as uncertainty about one's own identity. The decision rule that is used for this purpose, namely the maximin rule, yields unstable and highly implausible results when applied to real-world uncertainty,

To someone whose focus is set on the moral problems served at the philosophy department's seminar table, the inability of common moral theories to deal with risk and uncertainty may seem like one of the many small failures that keep the philosophical discussion alive and well. Unfortunately it is much worse than that. Outside of the seminar room, uncertainty about the effects of one's actions is a ubiquitous and often dominant element in the moral problems that we face in both private and public life. In order to make moral theory practically useful, we need to develop workable methods to analyse the ethical aspects of decisions under risk and uncertainty.

But before turning to that task, we should have a closer look at some of the basic problems that make a moral analysis of risk and uncertainty so difficult.

3
Back to Basics

In the previous chapter we saw that modern ethical theory has great difficulties in dealing with problems involving risk and uncertainty. The purpose of this chapter is to show that these difficulties are symptoms of fundamental deficiencies in the conception of human agency. We will start the diagnostic work by scrutinizing how the consequences of actions are delimited (Sections 3.1 and 3.2). This leads us to the core of the matter, namely the underlying view of causality (Section 3.3). The central claim of this chapter is that ethical thinking has been hampered by an outdated, pre-Newtonian view of causality that has largely been imported into ethics from decision theory (where it may be a more serviceable idealization). In order to deal satisfactorily with real-life problems such as those involving risk and uncertainty, ethical theory needs to develop an understanding of causality and consequentialness that is compatible with our knowledge of the physical world. In Section 3.4 some major implications for ethical theory of a more realistic view of causality are pointed out. Finally, Section 3.5 summarizes the lessons we have learnt in this and the previous chapter on how a moral account of risk should be constructed.

3.1 Delimiting consequences

An evaluation of risk-taking can be either process-oriented or outcome-oriented (or both). To exemplify this, consider a decision that Susan makes as the chief engineer of a major amusement park. Three days before the end of the season she discovers a faulty screw-bolt in the roller-coaster. She decides to run the coaster for the remaining three days, and orders thorough maintenance to be performed after the close-down.

Unfortunately, a major accident occurs on the very last evening of the season. Three persons fall off a wagon, and two of them are severely injured. In a process-oriented assessment of this event, the focus is set on the risk-taking as such. The evaluation refers to the moment at which the risk-taking took place, and its central issue is: Was it wrong to take the risk of running the coaster in spite of the faulty bolt? In an outcome-oriented assessment of the same event, the focus will be on the actual materialization of the risk, and on the negative outcome that actually occurred.

The difference comes out clearly in a discussion of the violation of rights. It would be reasonable in this case to say that the rights of the riders were violated. In a process-oriented assessment, we would say that the rights violation took place when Susan made her unfortunate decision. On that view, the violation was inherent in the very act of risk-taking. In an outcome-oriented assessment the violation would be considered to occur when the actual accident took place.

Modern ethical thinking is predominantly outcome-oriented. This applies not only in consequentialist ethics but to a large extent also in other moral theories. Irrespective of our choice of a moral theory, the categories under which actions are morally appraised usually refer to their consequences.[1] Hence, a deontologist's absolute prohibition to kill is an absolute prohibition to perform any action that has the death of another person as a consequence. The term 'outcome orientation' was chosen here in order to emphasize that the tendency it describes applies both to consequentialist and non-consequentialist ethics.

In everyday parlance, and mostly in moral philosophy, the terms 'outcome' and 'consequence' denote end states, i.e. such effects of an action or decision that still remain at the point in time referred to. To explain 'outcome' the Oxford English Dictionary uses phrases such as 'the way something turns out' and '[t]he product which results from an action, process, or system'. In colloquial usage, consequences are traces of something that happened previously. If there are no traces left of an action in the past, i.e. the world today is the same as it could have been if that action had not been performed, then it has no consequences any longer. However, it would be morally absurd to exclude all effaced consequences, such as forgotten suffering, from moral evaluation.[2] A plausible ethical theory should include effaced consequences in its moral appraisals. This can be done either by treating them as consequences or by evaluating them under some other designation.

Traditionally, consequences have been conceived as agency-excluding, i.e. describable without reference to the agency of past actions.

If I break an antique vase, then according to this view it is a consequence of that action that the vase has been broken, but it is not one of its consequences that the vase has been broken by me. Several authors have argued that this is a too limited notion of consequences. David Sosa noted that if an agent brings about the state *t* then the agent also brings about the complex state t^+ that includes *t* and also includes that she brings about *t*.[3] In a similar vein, Amartya Sen describes it as an 'odd surgery' to remove references to agency from the description of a state of affairs.[4]

Another potential delimitation of consequences concerns the motives and mental causes of actions. If I broke the vase intentionally, should the fact that it was broken intentionally be included in a description of its consequences? Motives and other action-accompanying states of mind have often been excluded from consequences. However, it is difficult to find a clear defence of this exclusion.[5]

In order to systematize the delimitation of consequences, it is useful to consider the relationship between the consequences and the causal effects of an action. Many utilitarians from Bentham onwards have at least implicitly identified consequences with causal effects. 'I think it is fair to say that almost all consequentialists mean by "consequences" the *causal* effects of actions. According to these views, an action is right if its *causal* net effect is better than the net effect of its alternatives.'[6] However, some modern, more elaborate versions of consequentialism identify the consequences of an action with a wider category of events that includes but is not exhausted by its causal effects.[7] The non-causal consequences of actions can be divided into two major categories.[8]

The first of these consists of that which '*must* obtain, if we are to say truly that the act has been done.'[9] The term 'direct consequences' can be used for this category. The direct consequences of an action consist of its causal effects and in addition everything else that must necessarily obtain if the cause produces these effects.[10] This includes the logical consequences of the causal effects. Hence, if I post a letter then it is a causal effect of this action that the letter is posted, and a direct (and logical) consequence that it is either posted or burnt.[11] The direct consequences may also include a wider category of states of affairs that obtain necessarily if the action is performed, but with a non-logical type of necessity. If I drop a fragile vase on the floor, then it is a causal effect of that act that the vase is broken. It is also a direct, but arguably non-logical, effect of this act that the vase was broken by me.[12]

The other category of non-causal consequences is those that follow necessarily from the combination of a casual effect and some contingent fact. These can be called combined consequences.[13] As an example, suppose that Anne invites John to dinner and that because John leaves the house, his mother spends the evening alone. Then it is a consequence of Anne's invitation that John's mother is alone, but this is not a direct consequence since it depends on contingent facts that are independent of the cause. A large part of the consequences that we refer to in everyday moral reasoning belongs to this category. They are characterized by following necessarily from the combination of the causal effects and some contingent fact that is suitable for such combinations.[14]

Two features of consequences that are important in moral philosophy come out clearly in this analysis. First, even though the consequences of an action do not coincide with its causal effects, they are generated by them. This makes consequences highly vulnerable to any problems or limitations in the notion of a causal effect. Secondly, the consequences of actions can be conceived more or less broadly. Conceptions of consequence can differ in their breadth (inclusiveness) while still relying on the same underlying notion of causality, depending on what contingent facts we consider suitable for forming combined consequences of a particular action.[15]

A broad view of consequences is often motivated by strivings to construct a consequentialist moral theory in which all morally relevant properties of an action are included in the evaluation of its consequences. A proponent of such a view might be tempted to refrain from any other restriction on the suitable contingent facts than that they should be true statements about the world in which the action takes place.[16] Unfortunately, although this construction has the virtue of simplicity, it yields blatantly implausible consequences. A few hours ago I lit a match in my home in Stockholm. At the same time, we may suppose, a violent fire broke out in a house in Kuala Lumpur. Then the following sentence is true: 'The match burns if and only if the house in Kuala Lumpur is on fire.' That the match burns is a causal effect of me lighting it. It would follow that it is a (combined) consequence of my act of lighting a match in Stockholm that the house in Kuala Lumpur is on fire.[17] This shows that some restriction is necessary on what contingent facts we can combine with a given action to obtain combined consequences. Otherwise the notion of consequences will become so broad that it is void of content.

Discussions of the breadth of consequences have mostly been couched in terms of the different variants of consequentialism that can be constructed with different delimitations of the consequences of actions. Proponents of broad consequentialism include a wide variety of an action's properties among its consequences.[18] Two major differences between a broad and a narrow interpretation are that the broad but not the narrow version includes (1) properties related to states of mind and (2) properties related to agents' adherence or non-adherence to moral and social rules.

Beginning with the former, if descriptions of the agent's mental state can be used to form combined consequences, then consequential evaluation can take the agent's motives and intentions into account. It can then make a difference in consequential terms, for instance, whether an assailant who killed his victim intended to do so. Of course, whether intentions are morally relevant and whether they are part of (or inferable from) an action's consequences are two separate questions. If the first question is answered affirmatively and the second negatively, then this will lead to a definition of consequentialism that makes it incomplete as a moral theory.

The second major issue is whether facts about the observance or non-observance of moral and social rules can be used to form combined consequences. If they can, then consequential evaluation can assign negative value to the breach of obligations and the infringement of rights. In this way, deontological and rights-based concerns can be included in consequential evaluation. This has often been seen as necessary to make consequential evaluation self-sufficient, or in other words to make consequentialism a plausible moral standpoint. David Sosa remarked that if an innocent person is hanged to create peace, then the consequences of this action include the violation of an innocent's rights.[19]

Some of the failures of traditional probabilistic risk analysis that we noted in Sections 1.1 and 2.2 can now be seen in a new light. Probabilistic risk analysis is usually presented as self-sufficient; its outcome is taken to tell us how serious a risk is. At the same time it represents an unusually narrow form of consequentialism, as can be seen from three notable omissions. First, it does not include *agency* among consequences. The negative value of a death or a harmful impact on health is the same irrespective of whose actions gave rise to it. This excludes important moral considerations. We would expect it to make a moral difference, for instance, if it is one's own life or that of somebody else that one risks in order to earn a fortune for oneself. [20] Secondly, the *mental states* of agents are excluded, among them states of mind that are highly relevant from a moral point of view such as intentionality and voluntariness. Most of us would not consider the act of throwing down a brick on a person from a high building to be morally equivalent to the act of throwing down a brick without first making sure that there is nobody beneath who can be hit by it (not even if both the probability and the severity of personal injury are the same for the two acts). Thirdly, *rule abidance* is excluded from consideration. This is problematic since a moral appraisal of a risk imposition would usually take into account whether the exposed person had a right not to be exposed to that risk.

There are two ways to deal with these deficiencies of traditional risk analysis. One option is to retain the narrow notion of consequences, but regard the analysis as an incomplete assessment that only covers some aspects of risk. It will then always have to be supplemented by a separate analysis that addresses issues such as agency, intentionality, voluntariness, and rule abidance.[21] The other option is to broaden the scope of consequences that are included in the probabilistic analysis. Then numerical values have to be assigned to factors such as voluntariness and infringements of rights. This will put an end to the conceptual simplicity (and apparent objectivity) that is a characteristic of current risk calculations.

3.2 Beyond broad consequences

According to broad consequentialism, if the consequences of actions are appropriately broadly defined, then they will cover everything that should be included in a moral assessment. This standpoint can be trivially confirmed by defining consequences so broadly that they include all properties of an action, or at least all properties that could at all be considered to be morally relevant. However, with such a broad definition, consequentialism will be a mere label with no contents at all.[22]

Can consequences at all be meaningfully delimited in a non-trivial way? In other words, are there morally relevant properties of actions that should not be reckoned among its consequences even on a reasonably broad view of consequences? As far as I can see, the best candidates for such non-consequential moral properties are those properties of an action that refer to the relations among various alternative developments rather than to what happens in each of these developments. For example, consider someone who risks a sleeping person's life by playing Russian roulette on her. In an assessment of this act, we need to consider (1) the set of consequences that will ensue if the person is killed, and (2) the set of consequences that will ensue if the person is not killed. In addition we should also take into account (3) the act of risk imposition, which in this case takes the form of intentionally performing an act that may result in either (1) or (2).[23] In many people's moral appraisal of this misdeed (3), the act of deliberate risk-taking, has considerable weight. It is perceived as a wrongdoing against the person that makes this act worse than the 'sixth of a homicide' that it could be described as in a simplistic probabilistic risk analysis.

This can be expressed with somewhat more precision as follows: In a consequential evaluation of (1) and (2), each of them will be replaced by its *closest deterministic analogue*.[24] (1) is then evaluated as the act of discharging a fully loaded pistol at the sleeping person's head and (2) as the act of letting off an unloaded pistol at her head. The composite act of performing what may turn out as either (1) or (2) is assumed to have no other *consequential* moral aspects than those that are present in one or both of the composite deterministic acts. The additional moral issues that are included in (3), i.e. the issues concerning risk-taking per se, are treated as non-consequential issues. Generally speaking, *those moral aspects of an act that are not present in the closest deterministic analogue of any of its alternative developments* can be regarded as essentially non-consequential. (These are process-oriented moral concerns in the somewhat looser terminology used in Section 3.1.)

The same delimitation can also be applied to a quite different problem, namely the evaluation of an opportunity set. We usually assign a positive value to an opportunity to choose. Having a choice between tickets to three attractive vacation trips is perceived as better than having a ticket to one of them (even if it is to the destination that one would choose among the three). Having a ticket to one of the three destinations is the closest deterministic analogue of the option to choose this destination among the three elements of the opportunity set. Therefore, the added value of the opportunity to choose is non-consequential according to the criterion just proposed. (This may contribute to explaining why it has been so difficult to account for opportunity sets in consequentialist frameworks.[25])

Of course, nothing important hinges on how we choose to define 'consequences'. My only worry is that if consequences are defined so broadly that they cover the (dis)value of risk-taking per se, then consequentialism becomes a weak and not very useful concept. The important conclusion to draw from this discussion is that a moral analysis of an action with uncertain outcomes has to include moral aspects that do not arise in an appraisal of the closest deterministic analogue of any of its alternative outcomes.

We now see a limitation in the formulation of the last chapter's mixture appraisal problem: A crucial assumption of that formulation is that an action under uncertainty can be decomposed into deterministic components, namely the closest deterministic analogues of each of its alternative developments. Furthermore, it is assumed that if we know the probabilities and the morally relevant properties of each of these components, then we can derive the value of the composite action. However, this method can only provide us with an incomplete moral appraisal since it does not cover the moral implications of risk-taking per se. Risk-taking is by definition not present in any of the deterministic components that are used in the analysis. This way of treating uncertainty, taking a (probabilistic) combination of alternative deterministic developments to hold all the information that is needed for the appraisal, is in fact the conventional procedure. It is inherent in the standard framework of decision theory, and it dominates in other areas that are strongly influenced by decision theory, including ethics. But as we have seen, it is incomplete. In order to avoid its deficiencies, it is necessary to give up the assumption that descriptions of the closest deterministic analogues of the possible outcomes of an action, each taken in isolation, contain all the information that is needed in a moral appraisal of that action.

3.3 Causality in reality

As we saw in Section 3.1, the consequences of an action depend both on its causal effects and on which contingent facts we allow to be used for the formation of combined consequences.[26] After investigating the selection of contingent facts, we should now turn to the notion of causality. All consequences of an action are consequences in virtue of something that is caused by that action. Therefore, the consequences of an action cannot be well-defined unless its causal effects (causal consequences) are well-defined, and in practice they cannot be known unless its causal effects are known.

Ethics is dominated by a simple and straightforward view of causality. It is the same view of causality that we use without reflection in everyday life and also in most other academic contexts. It conceives causality as consisting of binary cause-effect relations, relations of production. The hammer hits the nail and the nail is driven into the plank, hence the hammer-blow causes the movement of the nail. More complex processes are assumed to be describable in terms of chains of such cause-effect relationships.

The idea of a single cause producing an event is highly simplified. To begin with, the cause-effect relationships that we refer to – both in science and in everyday life – are highly idealized in the sense that they only mention one element of a set of conditions that are needed to produce the effect. The shutter release button of my camera went into two pieces when I pressed it only a couple of months after I bought the camera. Clearly, the break was caused by my act of pressing the button. However, when handing in the camera for warranty repairs, I was eager to point out that the button would not have broken under the light pressure of my finger unless there was some manufacturing defect. In my conversation with the shop attendant, I called this defect 'the cause' of the break.

This incident illustrates the simplification in ordinary causal talk that was brought to our attention by John Stuart Mill: Normally there are several causal factors that contribute to the production of an effect, but instead of dealing with them all on an equal basis we tend to select only one of them and call it *the* cause.[27] The remaining causal factors are treated as background conditions.[28] Our selection of 'the cause' depends on social conventions and is heavily influenced by context and purpose. We tend to select those causal factors as causes that are unexpected or considered to be deviant. '[T]he gas leak rather than the striking of a match is most usefully considered the cause of the explosion in a house, although the reverse would be true in a gas plant.'[29] In a course on microbiology we learn that cholera is caused by *Vibrio cholerae*. In a course on public health we learn that it is caused by lack of proper sanitation.[30]

The multiplicity of causal factors can at least in principle be dealt with by extending our descriptions of cause-effect relationships so that the whole set of causal factors is mentioned. Hence, in a causal explanation of a case of cholera, we can mention both the bacterium and the sanitary deficiencies. But the cause-effect model also has a much more serious problem that cannot be solved in that way. Although the model is adequate for describing many of the interrelations that apply in the real world, it is only a model, and as so often is true, the world does not conform perfectly to the model we use to describe it. There are many interconnections between events that cannot be adequately accounted for with this model. Bertrand Russell observed that 'oddly enough, in advanced sciences such as gravitational astronomy, the word 'cause' never occurs.'[31]

> 'In the motions of mutually gravitating bodies, there is nothing that can be called a cause and nothing that can be called an effect: there is merely a formula. Certain differential equations can be found, which hold at every instant for every particle of the system, and which, given the configuration and velocities at one instant, or the configurations

at two instants, render the configuration at any other earlier or later instant theoretically calculable.'[32]

The cause-effect pattern would have been sufficient for a full description of a clockwork universe in which all motions are produced directly by some other movement. This is the type of mechanistic model that can be found for instance in the natural philosophies of Robert Boyle and René Descartes, who assumed that natural phenomena can be described in the same terms as 'the movements of a clock or other automaton follow from the arrangement of its counter-weights and wheels.'[33] However, this is a pre-Newtonian model of the universe. The cause-effect pattern does not capture Newtonian physics, in which movements emerge from complex interactions between a large number of bodies, all of which influence each other simultaneously.

Modern physics is even less conformable to the cause-effect pattern than the physics that Russell referred to.[34] The experimental verification of quantum entanglement (the Einstein-Podolsky-Rosen paradox) shows that it is impossible to perform an isolated intervention in a subatomic system that influences only one other parameter.[35] Furthermore, since Russell published his paper, several other sciences have followed physics in adopting models in which the flow of events is determined by simultaneous mutual influences that are describable by systems of equations, rather than by the stepwise production of effects in a causal chain. This applies for instance to climatology, economics, and biological population dynamics. In other areas, such as political and organizational science, similar complex interactions are discussed although usually not in terms of equation systems.[36] In all these cases, an account restricted to binary cause-effect relationships will lack much of the explanatory power of modern science.[37]

But in spite of this, it is commonly assumed in moral philosophy that the long-term development of the world can be described in terms of long causal chains, in essentially the same way as if the world functioned like a complex clockwork, or a huge system of dominoes.[38] We have just seen that such a model is descriptively inadequate since the cause-effect pattern does not cover all connections that persist among events in the world. In addition, even when cause-effect relationships are in place, they need not be combinable into causal chains in the intended way. In other words, the cause-effect relationship is not in general transitive.[39] The presence of bacteria in an infected wound causes an increase in leukocytes, and the increase in leukocytes causes healing of the wound. However, the presence of bacteria in the wound does not cause its healing.

Of course, the cause-effect model is useful for many purposes, in particular within short time-spans. We can often describe some of the events that will take place soon after the performance of a single action fairly accurately in terms of cause-effect relationships. However, this does not mean that the development of the world 'consists' of cause-effect relationships, only that the cause-effect model is a useful approximation in these cases.

Some of the useful cause-effect relationships can in fact be derived from more general laws that do not conform to the cause-effect pattern. If we heat a gas in a closed container, then its pressure will increase. We can say that the raised temperature causes the heightened pressure. This is a cause-effect relationship that can be derived from a more general gas law. Its area of application is much more limited than that of the general law. If we want to describe complex processes involving gases with changing volumes, pressures, and temperatures, such as those in a heat engine, then we have to use the general law. A general gas law cannot be replaced by repeated applications of the simplified cause-effect relationships that are derivable from it.

Causality is often conceived as having the two properties of (1) being exhaustively representable by binary cause-effect relationships and (2) being universal, i.e. covering all the interconnections that there are between events in the world. As we have seen, this view of causality is not compatible with our knowledge about the structure of the world. We have to choose between two ways to make our concept of causality coherent.[40] We can define causality as composed of binary cause-effect relationships. Then causality cannot be universal. Alternatively we can use the term 'causality' in a wide sense that covers all the various types of interdependencies that obtain between events in the world. In the latter case, the structure of causality is a subject for empirical investigation rather than philosophical deliberation.

3.4 The (d)elusiveness of total consequences

Consequential evaluations of an action are often assumed to refer to its total consequences, i.e. the development of the world that will take place (indefinitely into the future) if it is performed.[41] In its simplest form, the notion of total consequences presupposes a deterministic model of the world in which causal chains continue indefinitely into the future. The most obvious problem with this simple model is that it cannot accommodate undetermined or random consequences. This is usually solved by introducing ramifying alternative developments, often with probabilities assigned to them. This corresponds to the insertion of random generators into the causal chain, transforming it into a branching causal tree. This model, the probabilistic version of the total consequences model, is essentially the model of the world employed in standard decision theory. It assumes that even if it is not knowable what will happen if one performs a certain action, there is at least a (possibly unknowable) truth in the matter – albeit only a truth about what will happen with what probability.

Even in its probabilistic version, the total consequences view presupposes that the future is determined by indefinitely linked action-consequence relationships. Since action-consequence relationships depend on underlying cause-effect relationships, they are subject to the same limitations in outreach that we have just found for cause-effect relationships. In practice this means that when the interconnections between events are well beyond the reach of cause-effect relationships, they are also inaccessible to action-consequence relationships. As an example, the execution of King Louis XVI had a major impact on European political history. The world would not have been the same today if it had not taken place. However, this action and its repercussions have been parts of a complex web of mutually influencing events. Therefore, its influence on present-day events cannot be described in terms of cause-effect or action-consequence relationships.[42]

It has often been pointed out that consequential evaluation is hampered by our inability to predict the consequences of our actions.[43] If the limitations of the total consequences view were merely epistemic, i.e. total consequences were well-defined but unknowable, then it might still have been a good strategy for moral analysis to search for the best approximation of this inaccessible truth. The criticism presented here is much more thorough-going, since it implies that the total consequences of actually occurring events are not even well-defined. This leaves us no choice but to reject the total consequences approach altogether.[44] It is not even an ideal that can be approximated.

Of course, the spuriousness of total consequences does not diminish the moral relevance of an action's foreseeable or probable consequences. I can have a duty to bring my wounded neighbour to the hospital, based on the expected effects of me doing so, even if there is no truth (not even an unknowable truth) about what will happen in the long run if I do it. Nevertheless, the limitations of the cause-effect model have important implications for how we should perform our moral appraisals. In particular, we have learnt that the consequences that an action has in isolation do not cover all the connections that it has with future events.

This gives us reason to take other types of interconnections into account in our moral deliberations.

The extension of moral analysis that this calls for is by no means an easy task. However, there is one comparatively easy step that we can and should take: Our moral appraisal of an action should include the consequences that the action can have in combination with other actions by the same or other agents, even if its contribution to these combined consequences cannot be isolated and evaluated separately. For a simple example of this, consider the action of flushing half a bottle of paint thinner down the toilet. Many would morally condemn that action because of its contribution to environmental contamination, although there is no harmful effect on the environment that is a consequence of it. Its wrongfulness is difficult to account for if we accept the currently dominant (albeit mostly implicit) assumption in moral philosophy that the moral status of a single action has to be derivable from the consequences of the action alone. But this is a standpoint that is based on a scientifically unrealistic view of how causality can be assigned.[45] A moral justification such as 'We all have to refrain from actions that contribute to pollution of the recipient of our sewage water' would be accepted in most colloquial moral discussions. It will have to be admitted in moral philosophy as well, provided that we adopt a more scientifically plausible view on causality and consequences. The demand that we should do our fair share in issues that concern many or all of us has a direct moral imperativeness that is not in need of being mediated by arguments referring to consequences of individual acts.[46]

3.5 Conclusion

This and the preceding chapter have been devoted to the somewhat unconstructive task of showing how and why current moral theories fail in the face of risk and uncertainty. The remaining chapters are devoted to the more constructive task of developing a plausible moral approach to risk and uncertainty. Some of the major lessons that we have learnt from previous failures can be summarized as follows:

1. The cause-effect and action-consequence relationships do not cover all the connections between an action and other events that are morally relevant.
2. In order to assess risk-taking or risk-imposing actions, it is not sufficient to consider the probabilities and values of potential outcomes.

We also have to take other factors into account, such as agency, intentions, and voluntariness.

3. Some of the relevant moral considerations in problems involving risk are not connected to any of the potential outcomes but instead refer to the very act of taking or imposing a risk. Therefore, separate evaluation of each possible outcome is not sufficient to cover the moral aspects that need to be taken into account.
4. Neither the disregard for persons (other than as carriers of impersonal value) that characterizes utilitarianism nor the veto for each concerned person conferred by major non-utilitarian moral theories is at all plausible. We need to develop a principled account that steers between these two extremes.

Part II
Making Prudent Risk Decisions

4
Reflecting on the Future

Many problems of risk are intricately combined with interindividual issues such as: When is it justified to expose someone else to a risk? When is a social distribution of risks fair? But there are also many problems of risk that do not involve any interindividual issues. Some risks concern only the person who takes them. Sometimes an agent acts unselfishly in someone else's interest. A group of persons can consider joint risk-taking in a situation where both risks and benefits will be shared equally. In all these cases, we can discuss which risks to take or accept without attending to traditional moral issues of conflicts between persons. This and the following chapter are devoted to risk problems of that type. Interindividual issues will be treated in Chapters 6 and 7.

A critic might question whether the issues selected for this and the next chapter at all belong to moral philosophy. The classification is inconsequential. We may call them issues of prudence in the old sense of that word, known from Aquinas, Hobbes, and others, that refers to wisdom and foresightedness in the furtherance of chosen ends (without the egoistic connotations that the word has in modern English).[1] At any rate the issues in question appear as components in more complex interindividual moral issues concerning risk and uncertainty. Moral philosophy needs ways to deal with them, irrespective of whether they are classified as internal or external to the discipline.

In this chapter, a framework for argumentation will be presented that can sharpen our moral intuitions in problems involving risk and uncertainty.[2] In Section 4.1 a simple but powerful argument pattern for reasoning about the future is drawn from colloquial, pre-theoretic moral argumentation, namely that we should think through beforehand how we will, in the future, view the decisions that we make now.

Here, this thought pattern is adapted to make it suitable for systematic moral appraisals of actions under uncertainty. Further elaborations are made concerning the specification of alternative future developments (Section 4.2), the value-base for assessing actions (Section 4.3), and the criterion by which alternatives are compared (Section 4.4). In the concluding Section 4.5, the method is summarized and its impact on the style of moral inquiry is characterized. In Chapter 5 it will be applied to different kinds of moral problems under risk and uncertainty.

4.1 The foresight argument

We need ethical thinking in our lives in order to go beyond the simple 'me now' perspective. We need to see our own actions in other personal perspectives than 'me' and other temporal perspectives than 'now'. This is what we teach our children when educating them to become responsible, empathetic, and thoughtful persons. We urge them to feel into other personal perspectives than the immediate 'me': 'Do not eat all the ice-cream. Think of how sorry Mary will be if there is nothing left for her.' We also urge them to feel into other temporal perspectives than the immediate 'now': 'Do not eat all your ice-cream now. Think of how sorry you will be tomorrow if there is nothing left.'

Moral philosophers have devoted considerable efforts to developing and advocating one of these two extensions of the ethical perspective, namely the use of other personal perspectives than 'me' to promote empathy. The moral usefulness of identifying oneself with other persons has been emphasized by philosophers at least since Mozi (Mo Tzu, 470–391 BC).[3] The same idea has also been expressed in many versions of the Golden Rule that have been attributed to religious leaders, such as 'Do not do to others what you do not want them to do to you'[4] (Confucius), 'All things whatsoever ye would that men should do to you, do ye even so to them'[5] (Jesus), and 'None of you truly believes until he wishes for his brother what he wishes for himself'[6] (Muhammed). Many of the argument patterns in modern moral philosophy can be seen as developments of the basic idea to put oneself in another's place. This applies, for instance, to moral arguments that employ ideal observers or hypothetical contracts.

Much less attention has been devoted to the other perspectives-extending practice, the contemplation of future perspectives to make ourselves more foresightful. It is the purpose of the present chapter to show how the simple everyday thought pattern just referred to can be fine-tuned to serve as a tool for the systematic assessment of moral problems involving risk and uncertainty.

One question comes up immediately: If we need methods to transcend both the 'me' and the 'now' perspectives, should we not attempt to use one and the same method for both purposes? Such a unified approach would follow the example of Parfit, who proposed that we treat our own future selves in the same way that we treat other people.[7] However, his proposal is based on a controversial and arguably counter-intuitive view of personal identity. Here, I will start from the common-sense experience that imagining one's own future thoughts and feelings is a quite different exercise from imagining what another person would think and feel. Similarities between interpersonal and intertemporal reasoning may (and will) emerge, but the thought pattern to be laid out here is general enough not to depend on contestable metaphysical assumptions about personal identity.

It is a good starting-point to consider the future-related arguments that we appeal to in supposedly deterministic settings. The basic type of argument that we are going to develop and refine can be called the foresight argument. It has the form of an attempt to see things the way that we will see them at some later point in time. Its simplest applications refer to situations that we treat as deterministic, such as the above ice-cream example. Another example may perhaps be closer at hand for some readers: Some of the consequences of drinking excessively tonight can, for practical purposes, be regarded as foreseeable. Thinking in advance about these consequences may well be what deters a person from drunkenness.

When the foresight argument is applied to cases with risk or uncertainty, more than one future development has to be taken into account. An example: Betty considers whether she should sue her ex-husband for having taken several valuable objects with him that she sees as her private belongings. This is no easy decision to make since her case is difficult to prove and she wants to avoid a conflict that may harm the children. When contemplating this she has reasons to ponder how she would react to each of the major alternative outcomes of the legal process. She also needs to think through how she would later look back at having missed the chance of claiming her rights. Generally speaking, in cases of risk or uncertainty there are several alternative 'branches' of future development.[8] Each of these branches can be referred to in a valid argument about what one should do today. The foresight needed to deal with such cases must therefore be applied to more than one future development.

As a first approximation, we wish to ensure that whichever branch materializes, a posterior evaluation should not lead to the conclusion that what we did was wrong. We want our decisions to be morally acceptable (permissible) even if things do not go our way. This can also be expressed as a criterion of decision-stability: Our conviction that the decision was right should not be perturbed by information that reaches us after the decision.

In this chapter, the foresight argument will be systematized into an argumentative procedure, *hypothetical retrospection,* in which alternative future developments are identified and comparatively assessed. The purpose is to morally guide our actions and decisions. But before going into the details of this procedure, its relation to regret-based argumentation needs to be clarified.

Colloquially, foresight arguments are often stated in terms of regret: 'Do not do that. You will regret it.' Related ideas in moral philosophy have often been expressed in terms of regret avoidance.[9] However, in a rigorous formulation, the foresight argument should not refer to regret. Regret is a psychological reaction, not an argued moral standpoint. Our moral aims when planning for the future cannot be condensed into an injunction to avoid such a psychological reaction. [10] Instead, we should aim at avoiding any future situation in which it will be our considered judgement that we should have acted otherwise. Such a situation is of course often accompanied by regret, but the two are not identical.

Two more specific reasons should be mentioned why predicted regret is not a suitable decision criterion. First, regret is compatible with the conviction that what one did was morally right.[11] This combination is to be expected when a person has been forced by circumstances to perform an action that would otherwise have been seriously wrong. An assaulted woman who killed her attacker in self-defence may well have feelings of regret and even guilt, even if she is convinced that she had no other means to rescue and that what she did was morally defensible. Or suppose that you decline an offer to invest your savings in a high-risk company, only to find out half a year later that the company has boomed and made all its shareholders rich. You may then regret that you did not invest in the company, while at the same time recognizing that at the time of the decision you did the right thing, given what you then knew.[12] It seems to be part of our normal functioning as human agents that we do not immediately and light-heartedly detach ourselves from the undesired effects of our actions even if we recognize them as necessary evils.[13]

Secondly, there are situations in which a person – at least one with certain psychological dispositions – may expect to feel regret whichever course she takes. If you bet on a horse and the horse wins, then you may regret not having placed more money on it. On the other hand, if it loses, then you may regret having placed money on it at all.[14]

The inadequacy of predicted regret as a decision criterion is not a new insight. Several authors seem to have approached decision criteria related to our notion of hypothetical retrospection, but they have backed off due to the implausibility of a regret-avoiding decision strategy.[15] In a workable specification of hypothetical retrospection, regret-based and other psychological criteria have to be replaced by criteria referring to the evaluator's considered moral judgement.

4.2 Specifying the branches

The conclusions drawn from a hypothetical retrospection will depend on how the ramified developments (branches) for evaluation are described and on what point in time is chosen for retrospective deliberations in those branches. Beginning with the former factor, in order to guide a decision, our deliberations should refer to branches that start out from a point representing the decision in question. Each branch has to be specified from this initial decision up to the moment at which the retrospection is enacted. This is important since the assessment should not be restricted to the end state (i.e. to effects remaining at the point in time of the hypothetical retrospection), but also cover the process leading up to it.

However, this initial decision need not be the only action to be included in the branches of future development that we construct for deliberation. As we saw in Section 1.5, deliberations on our (in)ability to control our future actions, and consequently our capacity to pursue plans, have a central regulating influence in our lives. We have to ask ourselves questions such as: Can I open the box of chocolates and take just one single piece? If I join my friend at the pub, will I return home sufficiently early and sober to finish the work that I promised to deliver early tomorrow morning? To accommodate such considerations in hypothetical retrospection, we need to construct branches containing more than one action by the agent.

A fair comparison between two alternative developments should be based on the same type of information about these alternatives. It is therefore highly desirable for the different branches under consideration to be specified in the same respects.[16] But unfortunately, this ideal can often not be fully achieved. In many of the decisions that we have to make, the choice of one alternative will lead to loss of information about the others.[17] We will never know what would have happened if we had chosen another education, another job, another partner, etc. The best that we can do to deal with this type of epistemic asymmetry is to combine a sufficiently late point in time for the appraisal with a sufficiently ramified presentation of the non-chosen alternatives. For an example of this, consider an academic's choice between a tenure-track position in a top-ranked university and a tenured position in a university considered mediocre. Her deliberations on these alternatives should reach sufficiently far into the future to cover the tenure decision in the first university. This yields three major branches, namely (i) going to the top university and obtaining tenure there, (ii) going to the top university and being dismissed several years later, and (iii) going to the lower-ranked university. If hypothetical retrospection is performed to guide this decision, retrospections should be enacted in each of these branches at some point in time when the tenure decision in the top university will have been made. Generally speaking, subdivisions of future developments should be so constructed that we avoid, as far as possible, comparisons between branches that differ widely in their degrees of uncertainty in issues that are crucial for the decision.

4.3 The value-base

After the branches and the point in time for hypothetical retrospection have been settled, the next step is to assess and compare the decision alternatives. Since hypothetical retrospection is not pre-committed to any particular moral theory, neither utilitarian calculations nor non-utilitarian considerations such as rights and duties are a priori excluded from these assessments. In particular, the framework allows for moral arguments that go beyond the traditional causal framework that was criticized in the previous chapter.

The purpose of hypothetical retrospection is to guide decisions. In order to guide a decision, a moral assessment has to refer to the conditions under which that decision is actually made. In particular, it has to refer to the information (actually) available at the time of the decision, not the information (hypothetically) available at some later point in time (such as the time at which retrospection is enacted). In other words, the decision-relevant moral arguments to be obtained from hypothetical retrospection are not of the form 'Given what I now know I should then have...'. Instead they have the form 'Given what I then knew, I should then have...'. This is another way in which hypothetical retrospection differs from decision-making based on predicted regret. Regret is often occasioned by information that we receive too late.

In the decisions and deliberations that I engage in at a particular point in time, I am committed to apply the moral values that I have at that point, since these are the only values that I am then bound by. There is no reason to apply moral values that one expects to acquire but does not presently endorse.[18] This applies equally to hypothetical retrospection. It has to be based on the values we have when we deliberate, not on the values we believe that we will have at the future point in time at which the deliberation is hypothetically enacted.

There is a further reason to base hypothetical retrospection on our actual values: We all have a tendency to acquiesce and to content ourselves with what the future brings us.[19] This is a mechanism of regret avoidance or dissonance reduction that seems quite functional. Without it, we would probably accumulate grievances to an extent that made our lives miserable. However, the values that we acquire as an appropriate posterior reaction to a misfortune are not necessarily the values on which we should base our still open choices that may influence whether such a misfortune will befall us. This was clearly pointed out by Henry Sidgwick, who noted that it is 'among the worst consequences of some kinds of conduct that they alter men's tendencies to desire, and make them desire their lesser good more than their greater'. To avoid this, he said, we should acknowledge 'that a man's future good on the whole is what he would now desire and seek on the whole if all the consequences of all the different lines of conduct open to him were accurately foreseen and adequately realised in imagination at the present point in time.'[20]

Thus, the hypothetically retrospective judgments that we are looking for will have to be (counterfactual) statements about the judgments that we would make at a future point in time if our values did not change. From a philosophical point of view, this requires a hypothetical temporal transference of values that may seem complicating.[21] From a practical point of view, this feature of hypothetical retrospection is simplifying. It would be difficult to reason under the hypothesis that one had different moral values than one has. This, fortunately, we have good reasons not to do.

4.4 The decision criterion

In hypothetical retrospection an action or decision is assessed in relation to the information that is available at the point in time when it takes place. This information will make it possible to relate each branch of possible development to other such branches. Therefore, our deliberations in hypothetical retrospection about a particular branch of development can be informed by comparisons to other alternative developments.

The procedure is in a sense doubly comparative: We do not first assess each branch separately, as if no other branch existed, and then only afterwards compare it to the others. Instead, the primary assessment of each branch is allowed to contain comparative judgements. Hence the final comparison takes place between objects whose assessment has already been influenced by comparisons. This may seem unduly duplicative, but it is necessary if we wish to take all the morally relevant information about the alternatives into account. Suppose that you have a choice between two action alternatives *X* and *Y*. If you choose *X* in this situation, then this is necessarily a choice not only of *X* but of doing-*X*-when-you-could-have-done-*Y*. This may be morally different for instance from doing-*X*-when-there-is-no-other-option, and also from doing-*X*-when-the-only-other-option-is-*Z*. The corresponding explication can be made of a decision in favour of *Y*. Therefore, a choice between *X* and *Y* is a choice between doing-*X*-when-you-could-have-done-*Y* and doing-*Y*-when-you-could-have-done-*X*. In particular, this is how we have to perform comparisons if we wish to take risk-taking per se into account (as argued for in Section 3.2). The riskiness (degree of risk-taking) of an alternative in a decision is not a property of that alternative in itself but of that alternative in relation to the other available alternatives.[22]

Although this way to perform comparisons (namely with alternatives that are inherently comparative) is unconventional from the viewpoint of standard decision theory, it conforms to the way in which we usually perform normative appraisals. The instruction 'assess normatively this course of action in a way that is independent of what its alternatives are' restricts the scope of the normative assessment since it requires that 'doing *X* when *Y* is the only other alternative' receives the same assessment as 'doing *X* when *Z* is the only other alternative'.[23]

The following example serves to illustrate the role of comparative judgements in hypothetical retrospection: A factory owner has decided to install an expensive fire alarm system in a building that is used only temporarily. When the building is taken out of use, the fire alarm has yet never been activated. The owner may nevertheless consider the decision to install it to have been right, since at the time of the decision other possible developments (branches) had to be considered in which the alarm would have been life-saving. This argument can be used not only in actual retrospection but also, in essentially the same way, in hypothetical retrospection before the decision. Similarly, suppose that there is a fire in the building. The owner may then regret that she did not install a much more expensive but highly efficient sprinkler system. In spite of her regret, she may consider the decision to have been correct since when she made it, she had to consider the alternative, much more probable development in which there was no fire but the cost of the sprinklers had made other investments impossible. Of course, this argument can be used in hypothetical retrospection just like the previous one. In this way, when we perform hypothetical retrospection from the perspective of a particular branch of future development, we can refer to each of the alternative branches and use it to develop either counterarguments or supportive arguments. In short, in each branch we can refer to all the others.

Hypothetical retrospection aims at ensuring that whatever happens, the decision one makes will be morally permissible from the perspective of actual retrospection. To accomplish this, the decision has to be acceptable from each viewpoint of hypothetical retrospection.[24] Another way to express this is that we aim for a decision, or choice of action, that is stable under the future developments that we can now foresee.[25] What makes this feasible is of course the fact that the assessment is doubly comparative in the sense explained above: Although each hypothetical retrospection takes a viewpoint in one particular branch of future development, from that viewpoint it deliberates on what one should have done, given the knowledge available at the point in time of the decision, and therefore it also takes into account the need to be prepared for the other branches.[26]

Arguably, full acceptability in all branches is not always achievable. The most problematic cases are conflict-ridden situations with high stakes. If a serious accident takes place that we had believed to be highly improbable, then we are almost sure to learn something from it, and see what we did before in a new light.[27] Only rarely would it be appropriate to say that enough had been done to prevent the accident from happening and that nothing should have been done differently. In order to achieve acceptability in this branch, we may have to take measures that would be so costly and cumbersome that they are unacceptable in at least some of the (perhaps much more probable) branches in which no accident of this type takes place. To the extent that this is foreseeable, we can also foresee that full acceptability in every branch is impossible to obtain.

Hence, we need a method to deal with cases in which full acceptability in all branches cannot be achieved. This can be done by treating them as a (generalized) form of moral dilemmas. A moral dilemma is a situation in which there is more than one alternative to choose between, but none of them is considered to be morally acceptable. Similarly, in the cases referred to here, there are several alternatives to choose between, but none of them is morally acceptable in all branches of future development. As I have argued elsewhere, even if a moral dilemma cannot be solved, we can make an optimal moral choice when confronted with it.[28] By this is meant that we choose an option that is not normatively inferior to any other option. (In some dilemmas, two or more alternatives satisfy this criterion, in others only one.) Similarly, if no alternative is available that is acceptable from every future viewpoint, then we should choose an alternative that comes as close as possible to that ideal. This means that we should determine the lowest level of unacceptability that some alternative does not exceed in any branch, and choose one of the alternatives that does not exceed it.[29]

This is not a maximin solution, i.e. it does not consist in choosing the alternative with the best security level.[30] To see this, suppose that an eccentric offers you a choice between a delicious apple and flipping a fair coin. If the coin yields heads, then you will receive a free trip to Hawaii. If it yields tails, then you will receive nothing. According to the maximin decision rule, you will have to choose the apple. Hypothetical retrospection tends to support the opposite conclusion. There are three branches to investigate, namely apple, coin-and-Hawaii, and coin-and-no-gain. If on the spur of the moment you choose the apple, then you are almost sure to think afterwards that you made the wrong decision since you missed the chance of winning the vacation trip. If you choose the coin flip but tails turns up, then you will probably consider the loss of the apple to have been worth the considerable chance of winning the trip. If the coin lands heads, then you will certainly consider your decision to have been the right one. All this can be foreseen in hypothetical retrospection, and therefore the outcome of these deliberations will expectedly lead you to choose the coin flip, contrary to the recommendations of the maximin rule.

In Section 4.2, criteria for the specification of branches were provided. However, there is a remaining problem: In complex decision issues, the number of potential branches of future development is so large that it will be impossible to attend to all of them. A selection of branches is necessary.

This selection should be based on a search for branches with a potential impact on the decision. We aim at choosing an alternative that is as defensible as possible in all branches of future development that can follow after it has been chosen. Therefore, we should attempt to find, for each alternative, those among its possible subsequent branches in which it is least defensible. In other words, for each alternative we should search for those branches in which the choice of this alternative will be most difficult to defend in hypothetical retrospection.[31] This refutationist approach can be summarized as a simple rule of thumb: 'For each alternative, find out when it would be most difficult to defend.'

For obvious practical reasons, the search for viewpoints suitable for hypothetical retrospection cannot reach indefinitely into the future. Fortunately, the proposed refutationist search procedure incorporates a mechanism that tends to restrict the time perspective. Due to the successive weakening of causal links, the effects of choosing one alternative in preference to another will become more and more uncertain and indeterminate as we go further into the future.[32] With this increasing uncertainty, the differences in value between alternative branches will in general decrease.[33] Therefore, the refutationist search procedure will in typical cases preclude excursions into the far-off future.

4.5 Conclusion

The basic principles of hypothetical retrospection can be summarized as follows:

> A hypothetical retrospection is an evaluation of a decision (action) or series of decisions (actions) in relation to the available alternatives. It is hypothetically enacted at some future point in time in any of the branches of possible future developments following after the decision.
>
> A hypothetical retrospection refers to a branch of future development in its full length up to the moment at which the retrospection is enacted, hence covering not only the outcome but also the process leading up to it. It is based on the moral values that the deliberator has at the time when the actual deliberation takes place. Its outcome is an evaluation of the decision(s) or action(s) in this branch as seen in relation to their alternatives and to what the agent was justified in believing at the time(s) of decision (action).
>
> Moral deliberation under conditions of risk or uncertainty should include a systematic search for future viewpoints for hypothetical

> retrospection. The major guiding principle in this search should be to find, for each alternative, the future developments under which it would be most difficult to defend morally in hypothetical retrospection. Branches and times for evaluation should be selected to make the assessed branches as comparable as possible in terms of the information available for assessment.
>
> If there is an alternative that comes out as morally acceptable (permissible) in every hypothetical retrospection that is enacted from a viewpoint at which this alternative has been chosen, then such an alternative should be chosen. Otherwise, an alternative should be chosen that does not in any hypothetical retrospection exceed the lowest level of unacceptability that some alternative does not exceed in any hypothetical retrospection.

Hypothetical retrospection is presented here as a basic standard for moral deliberation under risk and uncertainty. In order to facilitate its practical use, a procedure for collective deliberation has been constructed that approximates its deliberative ideals.[34] Hypothetical retrospection can also be simplified to a risk manager's rule of thumb: 'Make a decision that you can defend also if an accident happens.'

It might be contended against this whole proposal that hypothetical retrospection adds nothing of importance to the process of moral appraisal. Since the retrospective assessment concerns the decision that one is about to make, and assumes the knowledge and the values that one actually has, why take the trouble of going mentally 'forwards and backwards' in time to make this assessment? Why not reason directly about the alternatives instead of pondering how one would judge them in a perspective of hindsight?

My answer to this is that the realism induced by constructing scenarios for hindsight adds seriousness and concreteness to our moral deliberations. Moral reflection is made more foresightful by simulating the effects of afterthought. These effects are to some extent analogous to those of systematically considering one's moral decisions from the perspective of other concerned individuals. Doing so is by no means a panpharmacon that solves all moral problems; rather it is the first condition for moral thinking about interpersonal issues. In the same way, systematically considering alternative future perspectives may well be a first condition for moral thinking about the uncertain future.

Contrary to many other proposed frameworks for ethical reasoning, hypothetical retrospection applies moral intuitions in a systematized way directly to actual moral problems, rather than using intuitions to derive rules that will in their turn be applied to real moral problems in a second phase of moral discourse. Although it draws upon the reasoner's capacity for imagination and hypothetical reasoning, it does so only in order to invoke fully realistic situations for moral appraisal, namely situations that represent possible future developments.[35] The concreteness gained in this way has the advantage that our moral deliberations will be based on 'the full story' rather than curtailed versions of it. More specifically, this procedure brings to our attention the interpersonal relations that are often left out in other accounts of risk, such as who exposes whom to a risk and who receives the benefits.

The form of moral reasoning represented by hypothetical retrospection should not be confused with an atheoretical approach that does not go beyond what is immediately given. In order to make the intended deliberative use of our moral appraisals of realistic situations, we need (1) systematic procedures for finding relevant and realistic scenarios, such as the refutationist search procedure described above, and (2) an account of the various types of moral arguments that can validly be used within this framework for comparing and combining the insights gained from different scenarios. To such arguments we will now turn.

5
Thinking in Uncertain Terms

The previous chapter introduced a general thought pattern, hypothetical retrospection, for moral deliberation on problems involving risk and uncertainty. In the present chapter, this thought pattern will be used to develop and justify some more specific argument forms for risk and uncertainty. Here as well, we will leave out interindividual issues such as justice and conflicts of interest. More precisely, we will assume that the action or decision under consideration is performed for the furtherance of only one interest (that may be the interest of a single individual or the joint interest of several individuals). Interindividual issues are deferred to Chapters 6 and 7.

In Section 5.1, the proper use of expected utility maximization is delineated, and three conditions of applicability for this method are proposed. In Section 5.2, the general effects of uncertainty on a moral appraisal are discussed, and it is explained how and why uncertainty tends to increase our moral leeway. Section 5.3 discusses in some detail the effects on a moral decision of uncertainty about the probabilities that are relevant for the decision. Section 5.4 explores the moral relevance of mere possibilities of untoward events. The major conclusions from this chapter are summarized in Section 5.5.

5.1 The proper use of expected utility

In previous chapters warnings were raised against some unreflected applications of probabilities and probability estimates.[1] It is equally important to warn against decision methods that disregard decision-relevant probabilistic information. (The maximin rule is the most well-known decision rule that answers to that description.)

> *Example 5.1:*
> You and your family have been offered to borrow a house at the seaside over the weekend. You know from previous experiences that the outcome of such a trip will depend on the weather. If it rains, then your weekend will be slightly worse than if you had stayed at home. If it does not rain, then it will be much better than if you had stayed at home.
>
> *Case i:* According to the weather forecast on Friday afternoon, the probability of rain during the weekend is about 5 per cent.
>
> *Case ii:* According to the weather forecast on Friday afternoon, the probability of rain during the weekend is about 95 per cent.

If you make this decision with a rule or procedure that disregards probabilities, then you will have to make the same decision in the two cases. This is a highly implausible restriction. Most of us would go to the seaside in case *i* but stay home in case *ii*. This can easily be justified in hypothetical retrospection. Let us look at the crucial eventualities. Suppose that in case *i* you go to the seaside, and the unlikely happens, namely steady downpour in spite of the optimistic prognosis. In retrospect, you will probably still consider the decision to go to the seaside to have been right, since for all that you knew a more positive outcome was much more probable. On the other hand, suppose that for some reason you decide to go to the seaside in case *ii*, i.e. with the pessimistic weather prediction. No convincing posterior defence of such a decision seems to be available, under the assumptions given in the example. Similarly, suppose that you stay in town and then receive information on Sunday afternoon that the weather has been excellent at the seaside. In case *ii*, but not in case *i*, you can easily defend your decision by noting that when you made it you had no reason to act under the presumption of good weather.

This is all rather trivial. Our everyday actions and decisions are unceasingly influenced by our judgements of how likely different outcomes are. These judgements are usually not expressed in exact numerical terms, and in many cases we would not be much helped by numbers. In Example 5.1 it makes no difference if we replace 5 per cent by 'very improbable' and 95 per cent by 'very probable'. It is, in fact, in such terms rather than in terms of numerical probabilities that uncertainties are usually expressed in weather forecasts. Even when no numerical probability estimates are available, judgements of comparative likelihood may be serviceable for decision guidance.

But in addition to that, can the standard decision-theoretical use of numerical probabilities, namely the maximization of expected utility, be justified in the framework of hypothetical retrospection? It turns out that it can, but only under certain conditions and not as a universal rule for all types of decision-making. Expected utility maximization seems to be justifiable in the following case:

> *Example 5.2:*
> A country is going to decide whether or not it will make the use of seat belts compulsory. Calculations based on extensive experience from other countries show that the expected number of deaths in traffic accidents is 300 per year if safety belts are compulsory and 400 per year if they are optional.
> The sole aim of the decision is to reduce the total number of traffic casualties.

Under the assumptions of this example there could not be much doubt that seat belts should be made mandatory. This can easily be corroborated with hypothetical retrospection. If we refrain from mandating seat belts, then about 400 people a year will be killed, and we will know that with another decision that number would have been about 300. Since this decision had the sole purpose of reducing the number of victims of death on the road, it cannot reasonably be defended in retrospect. (A justification would have to refer to aims or considerations that were excluded in the assumptions of this example, such as the right of individuals to choose freely whether or not to use a seat belt.)

It is important to recognize that this argumentation is based on the assumption that outcomes can be appraised in terms of a single number (in this case the number of persons killed) and that this number is all that counts. This assumption is usually made in discussions of road safety, but it is by no means incontestable.

> *Example 5.3:*
> A new steering device makes it possible for drivers to steer to the side much faster, for instance in order to avoid a head-on collision. The voluntary introduction of this device in several car models has provided statistical information about its effects on casualties. Therefore, the effects of its general introduction can be prognosticated. It will lead to a significant decrease in the number of motorist and passenger fatalities. However, since drivers tend to drive faster when they have this device, it will also lead to a larger number of

pedestrian fatalities. About 200 motorists and passengers will be saved, but about 100 more pedestrians will be killed, more than half of which will be children. This adds up to a net decrease in deaths of about 100. Should the new steering device be introduced in all new cars?

Although the reduction in fatalities is the same here as in Example 5.2, this example is much more problematic. Here, we cannot avoid issues of justice. Is it really fair to provide motorists with a tool that reduces their own risks but instead puts unprotected children at greater risk? Can the loss of a certain number of innocent children be justified by saving a larger number of motorists who choose to drive dangerously? Without going into any details about this, we can conclude that the simple solution to base the decision just on the net gain of 100 lives is only available if justice and other interindividual issues are disregarded or considered irrelevant.[2]

Furthermore, the argumentation in Example 5.2 depends on the large number of road accidents that levels out random effects in the long run. It is due to the law of large numbers that we know that about 100 more persons per year will be killed if seat belts are not compulsory. When the numbers are large, the expected utilities will become actual in the form of average utilities. The same type of argument cannot be used when this condition is not satisfied, in particular not in case-by-case decisions on unique or very rare events.[3]

Example 5.4:[4]

A trustee for a minor empties her bank accounts and buys shares for her in a promising company. He has good reasons to believe that with this investment the statistical expectation value of her fortune when she comes of age will be higher than if her money had remained in the bank accounts.

Half a year later, the company runs into serious trouble, and the shares lose most of their value within a few days. When the trusteeship ends, the beneficiary's fortune is worth less than a tenth of its original value.

It would not be easy to defend this failed investment in retrospect. The law of large numbers is of no help here since, contrary to the seat belt example (5.2), there is no collection of similar cases that this trusteeship can be combined with, yielding a positive result in the long run. If the beneficiary had a multitude of fortunes, it would arguably be best for her to have them all managed according to the principle of maximizing expected utilities (provided of course that the risks connected with the different fortunes were statistically independent). But she had only one fortune, the one that the trustee squandered.

As this example shows, the justification of expected utility maximization requires that an action-type or type of decision is repeated sufficiently many times to put the law of large numbers into operation. The justification then refers primarily to the large-scale decision to apply expected utility maximization in the many small decisions or actions, and only derivatively to its application in the individual cases. Therefore, the justification of expected utility maximization is sensitive to how decisions are framed. Its application in a single decision is only justified if that decision is included in a sufficiently large group of decisions for which a justified metadecision to maximize expected utility is adhered to. As an example, a case can be made that the regulation of safety equipment in motorcars should be based on the maximization of expected utility (minimization of expected damage). The consistent application of this criterion in all the different specific regulatory decisions would minimize the damage caused by technical failures of motor vehicles. The larger the group of decisions that are covered by such a rule, the more efficient is the levelling-out effect, i.e., the larger catastrophic consequences can be levelled out.

Given this, cannot we justify expected utility maximization as a universal rule? Cannot we just combine decisions and actions into sufficiently large groups, perhaps into one single group consisting of all human decisions? Some reflection will show that this does not work in practice. As we have already seen, expected utility maximization cannot be used when we have to take into account the interests or welfare of more than one person or group, and these several interests are not reducible to a single number. All major areas of social decision-making seem to include recalcitrant conflicts of interest. This makes it impossible to form large groups of issues in which all decisions can be appraised according to one and the same, one-dimensional criterion. Without such a reduction, the justification of expected utility maximization does not go through.

In addition, there is an absolute limit to the levelling-out effect and therefore also to the justification of expected utility maximization. Very large negative effects, such as a nuclear war or a major ecological threat to human life, cannot be levelled out even in the hypothetical limiting case in which all interindividual issues are disregarded, and all human decision-making is subsumed under a one-dimensional numerical criterion. The Pentagon is known to have used expected utility calculations in the calibration of command and control devices for nuclear warheads (based on secret utility assignments to an accidental nuclear strike and to a failure to respond to a nuclear attack).[5] Such usage of expected utility seems to go beyond what can be justified by the levelling-out effect. The same is true of the application of expected utility to risks of large-scale ecological threats to the inhabitability of the Earth. In cases like these, the levelling-out effect required to justify expected utility maximization would only come forth in the perspective of the Norn who sees many worlds come and go.[6] This is not the perspective in which we humans should see our own decisions and actions.

One further problem in expected utility maximization requires our attention. In the above examples, it was assumed that reliable probabilities are available. But as we saw in Section 1.2, probabilities are in practice always subject to some degree of uncertainty. The simplest and by far most common approach to this uncertainty is to identify what one believes to be the most credible probability assessment and then rely on that assessment in the analysis. Unfortunately, this approach sometimes leads us wrong.[7]

> *Example 5.5:*
> Peter agrees to Alice's proposal that they toss a coin to decide who shall do a tedious cleaning task in their amateur theatre club. Then he pulls out a coin from his inside pocket, hands it over to her and says: 'Let us use this coin. You throw it.' Alice recalls that Peter is an amateur magician. It occurs to her that his coin may be biased.
> *Case i*: Peter continues: 'You choose whether heads or tails means that you win and I do the cleaning.'
> *Case ii*: Peter continues: 'If it lands heads up, then you do the cleaning. If it lands tails up, then I will do it.'

In case *i*, Alice may well agree to Peter's proposal (provided that she has some means to choose between heads and tails without being influenced by him). Admittedly, if the coin is biased and she has bad luck in her choice of a side of the coin, then the probability that it lands on the unfavourable side may be well above 0.5. But it is equally likely that the toss will be as much biased in her favour. If she agrees to the proposal and loses, then this decision will be easy to defend in retrospect since there was no alternative available that would yield a better chance of success. Case *ii* is quite different. Here, the possibility of a bias to her disadvantage is not balanced by an equally likely possibility of a bias to her advantage. She therefore has a good reason to reject the proposal.

Generally speaking, the probabilities on which we base expected utility calculations have *symmetric error tendencies* if over- and underestimates of the same size are equally likely. In that case, the uncertainty of the probability estimate has no impact on the expected utility. We can then safely disregard the uncertainty and base our analysis exclusively on the central, most credible estimate. However, if there is asymmetry in this respect, then an expected utility based on the central estimate may be misleading.

Unfortunately, asymmetric error tendencies are the rule rather than the exception in wide areas of application. This is, for instance, true of estimates of the probabilities of accidents. Consider an estimate that the probability of an explosion in a certain pressure vessel in the next year is 10^{-5}. For this probability to have a symmetric error tendency, it should be the case for each probability increment d that it is equally likely that the true probability is $10^{-5}+d$ and that it is $10^{-5}-d$. But clearly this cannot be, as we can confirm by setting $d = 2\times10^{-5}$. The estimated probability can be that much too low (i.e. the correct value may be 3×10^{-5}), but it cannot be that much too high (since the correct value cannot be negative). Due to this asymmetry, a decision based exclusively on the central, most probable estimate can be expected to be more risk-prone than the 'risk-neutral' ideal of maximized expected utility. (In some cases this problem can be solved with a recalculation using second order probabilities to arrive at a new probability estimate with a balanced error tendency.[8])

In conclusion, we have identified three applicability conditions that must all be satisfied for expected utility maximization to be justified: (1) There should be no conflicts of interest or issues of justice that need to be taken into account. (2) One and the same type of action or decision is repeated sufficiently many times to make the law of large numbers applicable. (3) The probability estimates have balanced error tendencies.

5.2 Uncertainty and moral leeway

We will now shift the perspective from probabilities to uncertainties. Obviously, uncertainty about the various factors that may have influence on our moral appraisals can make us more uncertain about these appraisals. As we will now see, uncertainty can also have other, less obvious effects on moral appraisals. Consider the following example:

Example 5.6:
Robert is at the ticket office to buy tickets to the opera as a surprise present for his wife who loves opera but has not seen one for many years. The theatre runs two productions, Verdi's *La Traviata* and Wagner's *Tristan und Isolde*. Robert wants to choose the play that his wife will like the most, but since he knows virtually nothing about opera, this is difficult for him.

Case *i*: He knows that Wagner is her favourite composer.

Case *ii*: He has no clue as to which opera she may like the best.

Given the purpose of his choice, it is fairly obvious that in case *i* Robert should buy tickets for *Tristan und Isolde*; whereas, in case *ii* he may choose either play. This illustrates a very general principle: Uncertainty tends to reduce moral requirements and thereby increase the moral leeway, or moral latitude, so that a larger selection of permissible alternatives is open to the agent. The mechanism behind this phenomenon is fairly simple: The moral status of an action is to a large degree determined by empirical circumstances including (but not necessarily restricted to) its consequences. Uncertainty consists in a wide epistemic scope, i.e. a wide scope of potential beliefs that you can legitimately hold or at least take to be serious possibilities. The moral status of the action will be different for different such beliefs, and therefore the moral scope is usually widened when the epistemic scope is widened. This can be called the principle of uncertainty transduction, since it consists in uncertainty being transduced from the empirical to the moral realm.[9]

The following case is less clear than the two previous ones:

Example 5.6, continued:
Case *iii*: Robert does not know his wife's attitudes to Wagner or Verdi. However, the ticket clerk tells him that Wagner was a German composer whereas Verdi was an Italian. Robert vaguely recalls that his wife's favourite composer is another German by the name of Bach.

In this case Robert may take the information from the ticket clerk as an indication that his wife likes Wagner's music. However, the indication is quite weak (and may well be misleading). A good argument can be made that this indication is too weak to be compelling and that he therefore has the same scope of permissible actions as in case *ii*. If he picks the Verdi performance, and later learns that his wife would have preferred *Tristan und Isolde*, he does not in retrospect have any reason to consider his choice to have been wrongful. Contrary to case *i*, he has good reasons to claim that he had no reasonably reliable information in the matter, and that the inkling he got from her preference for that other German composer was just a hunch of a kind of that one often does wisely to neglect.

Uncertainty transduction is not the only source of moral leeway. Even the most exacting moral theories grant us moral liberty to choose between alternative courses of action that rank equally high in the moral appraisal, and this even in fully deterministic situations. Some moral theories also allow us to choose between alternatives that differ in their value but are nevertheless all acceptable.[10] Uncertainty transduction is an additional source of moral leeway. Due to the prevalence of uncertainty in our lives, it probably contributes much to the moral leeway that we consider ourselves to have, although it is so ingrained that we seldom think about it.

Uncertainty transduction is equally important in social and political life as in our personal lives. In most public debates, the contestants disagree at least as much on the effects of various proposed courses of action as they disagree on the ultimate values. The political development of the climate change issue is an interesting example of the policy impact of different degrees of uncertainty. A comparison between the first Assessment Report by the IPCC (International Panel on Climate Change) in 1990 and their fourth Assessment Report in 2007 does not show any large differences in their estimates of the most probable development of the future climate.[11] The major difference between the two reports is a significant reduction in the uncertainty of the estimates. It was this reduction in uncertainty more than anything else that gave rise to some political action.

Finally, it should be emphasized that although uncertainty tends to increase the moral leeway, this is not a universal law. When arguments supporting two different alternatives balance each other out, increased uncertainty may well derange the balance in favour of one of the alternatives, thus leading to a smaller rather than a larger moral leeway.

Example 5.7:
An industrial company has the choice between two cleaning agents *A* and *B*. Since they do not differ in price or technical performance, this choice depends only on two factors, namely flammability and toxicity.

Case i: It is known that *A* is more flammable than *B*. Nothing is known about the toxicity of the two substances.

Case ii: It is known that *A* is more flammable than *B*. Furthermore, toxicity data is available for the two substances, showing that *B* is moderately toxic but giving no indication that *A* is toxic.

In case *i*, there can hardly be any doubt that *B* should be chosen rather than *A*. With the additional information available in case *ii*, the advantage of *B* in terms of flammability and that of *A* in terms of toxicity may turn out to have equal weight. If this is so, then a choice of *A* is equally justified as a choice of *B*. In that case, a reduction in uncertainty gives rise to a larger moral leeway, contrary to the general tendency.

5.3 Uncertainty about probabilities

The probability estimates on which we base our decisions can be more or less uncertain.[12] Uncertainty transduction operates also on this type of uncertainty, uncertainty about probabilities. If a moral argument is based on a probability estimate, then that argument is weaker the more uncertain the probability estimate is. When a probability-based argument is weakened, then the relative importance of other, non-probabilistic arguments tends to increase.

Example 5.8:
A physician has the choice between two drugs that she can prescribe to patients with a certain condition. She has long experience with drug *A*, but learns that some colleagues have started to use drug *B* instead. In a medical journal she reads that a scientific committee has recently issued a comparative report. According to that report, *B* has the same low risks of side-effects as *A*. A significant clinical improvement has been found in 84 per cent of the patients taking *B* but only in 69 per cent of the patients taking *A*.

Case i: The medical journal continues to report that there is consensus among leading clinical experts that the conclusions of this report are correct.

Case ii: The journal reports that leading clinical experts are unwilling to draw definite conclusions from this report. 'I agree that these are the best estimates available', said one of these experts, 'but they are based on much fewer patients than what we need to draw reliable conclusions in the matter'.

Suppose that our physician prescribes drug *A* in this situation. A patient whose condition was not improved by the treatment can then complain that another treatment was available with only about half the risk of this happening. In case *i*, the physician has no good defence against such an accusation. She could have acted in a way that had given the patient a better chance of recovery, and she did not have a good reason not to do so. However, in case *ii* she would have a good defence, namely that the new information was so uncertain that she was justified in relying more on her own clinical experience with drug *A*. Hence, due to uncertainty transduction, a decision to continue prescribing *A* would pass the test of hypothetical retrospection in case *ii* but not in case *i*.

This example also serves to introduce an application area in which uncertainty about probabilities has a central role, namely the justification of clinical trials.[13] A clinical trial is a treatment experiment in which patients with the same condition are randomized between different regimens in order to determine which of these has the best overall effects. Such trials give rise to an immediate ethical problem: How can the randomization of patients between treatments be morally justified? Should not every patient be offered the treatment that is best for her, according to the best clinical judgment? In order to answer this question, we need to consider the uncertainty associated with probabilistic information about treatment effects.

A full discussion of the justification of clinical trials would have to take interpersonal issues into account. (Can advantages to future patients justify disadvantages befalling current patients?) It would also have to consider the roles of patients and physicians in clinical decision-making (and in particular the requirement of the patient's informed consent to any clinical intervention). Here, in order to focus on uncertainties about probabilities, such issues will be disregarded. To achieve this, we will place ourselves in the role of a physician who has to decide whether it is in a particular patient's interest to be included in a clinical trial.

The most common defence of clinical trials refers to the uncertainty about treatment effects that prevails when the trial is conducted. A patient should not be offered to participate in a trial if it is known beforehand that one of the trial treatments is worse for her than the other, or worse than some other treatment that is available in clinical practice. Hence, a clinical trial can only be justified if there is uncertainty about treatment effects. The uncertainty should be such that either treatment would be a reasonable and defensible choice, given the available information. Such a situation has been called 'equipoise' or 'clinical equipoise'.[14]

Equipoise can be accounted for in terms of the probabilities of different treatment outcomes. For simplicity, I will assume that treatment outcomes can be represented in one dimension. This is of course a simplification. Basically, treatment outcome is multi-dimensional. After a few days of treatment with an antibiotic, a pneumonia patient may have improved lung function, unchanged erythrocyte sedimentation rate, worse diarrhoea, etc. However, in clinical practice the various symptoms are usually combined into an overall summary of the patient's condition. It is taken to be conceptually unproblematic to summarize the overall development of a patient's health as improved, unchanged, or worsened. In what follows, I will adhere to this practice.

Given such a unified measure of treatment effects, our expectations on the outcome of a specific treatment on an individual patient can be expressed in probabilistic terms as in Figure 5.1. The x-axis represents the overall treatment effect, with better outcomes to the right and worse outcomes to the left. The y-axis represents probability. The curve shown in the figure represents the probability distribution of the outcome of a particular treatment.

A distribution such as that in Figure 5.1 is always relative to the available knowledge. For every specified treatment and patient group there is, in principle, a true probability distribution that corresponds to perfect knowledge about the relative frequencies of different treatment outcomes. In practice, what we have access to are estimates that can be based on anything from extensive previous clinical trials to uncertain interpretations of animal experiments. Typically, we should expect the estimates to be uncertain for new drugs, and the corresponding distribution curves will be quite wide. As evidence accumulates, the estimates become less uncertain and the distribution curves will be narrowed down.

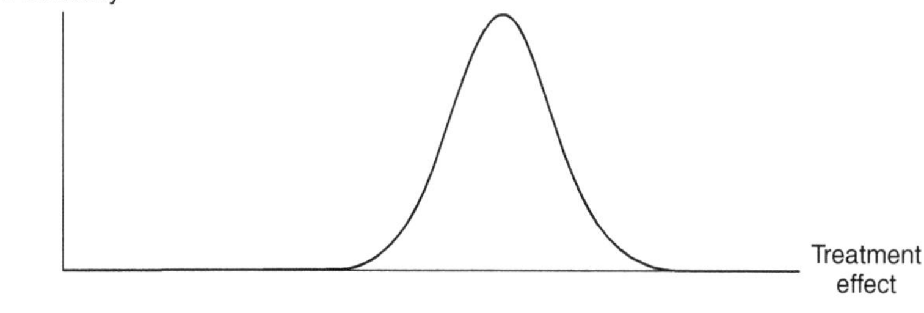

Figure 5.1 The probability distribution of the overall treatment effect of a drug

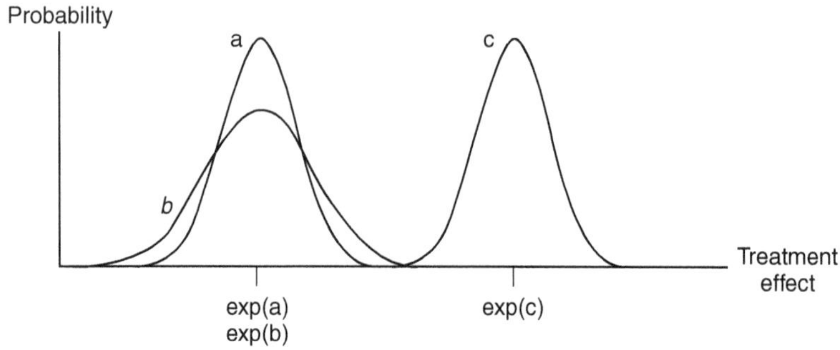

Figure 5.2 Distribution curves for three drugs

For simplicity of illustration, I will assume that the top of the distribution curve represents the expectation value of the treatment effect.[15] As can be seen in Figure 5.2, one and the same expectation value can be associated with greater or smaller uncertainty. Here, the tops of the two distributions *a* and *b* have the same projection (*exp*(*a*) = *exp*(*b*)) to the x-axis. This means (with the assumption just made) that they have the same expectation value. However, *b* is a wider distribution that represents a much higher degree of uncertainty. The third distribution, *c*, represents much better treatment outcomes than *a* or *b*, with the same degree of uncertainty as *a*. Among these three treatments, *c* would be the obvious choice.

Figure 5.3 shows a prototypical situation for a clinical trial. Here, *d* represents the standard treatment that is used in current clinical practice, whereas *e* represents a new, experimental treatment. In order to show that there is equipoise between *d* and *e*, we can compare them in an ordinary clinical context, i.e. as treatments offered to patients in routine care and not as (randomized) alternatives in a clinical trial. For that purpose, suppose that as a patient you are given the choice between these two treatments. The choice would not be easy. You have a good reason to choose *e*, namely that its expectation value *exp*(*e*) is better than the expectation value *exp*(*d*) of *d*. But you also have a good reason to choose *d*, namely that its worst outcome *min*(*d*) is better than the worst outcome *min*(*e*) of *e*.

This can be further corroborated with hypothetical retrospection. For the reasons explained in Section 4.4, we can focus on the worst cases that can ensue after choice of *d* or *e* respectively. First consider

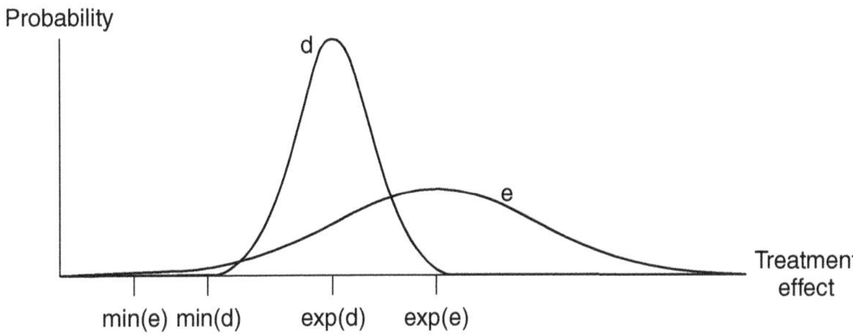

Figure 5.3 Distribution curves for two drugs

the case in which you chose *d* and the outcome is *min*(*d*). Among the various outcomes that are possible after choosing *d*, this is of course the one that will make the choice most difficult to defend. Someone might argue that the decision was wrong since you would have had a very good chance of a better outcome if you had chosen *e*. However, this argument can be confuted by pointing out that if you had chosen *e* then you might have fared even worse: You could then have met with the treatment outcome *min*(*e*). Next consider the other difficult case, namely that in which you chose *e* and the outcome is *min*(*e*). Someone might argue that this decision was wrong since if you had chosen *d* you would have obtained a better outcome. However, this argument can be contravened by pointing out that you only had extremely bad luck. When you made the decision, the expected outcome from *e* was much better than that from *d*.

Thus in both cases, both if you choose *d* and if you choose *e*, you have a reasonable defence for your choice. This is because there are two competing criteria for choosing between the two probability distributions. It is reasonable to prefer the distribution with the highest expectation value, but it is also reasonable to prefer that which has the highest security level. When these two arguments point in different directions, they must be weighed against each other, and in some cases they will balance each other out. There are no exact and predeterminable decision-weights for weighing them against each other. Instead, we can think of decision-makers as (collectively and individually) indecisive within a range of reasonable decision-weights for this purpose. This indecisiveness gives rise to a moral leeway. The equipoise required for clinical trials can only arise when we are within the range of that leeway, i.e. the range in which both distributions are eligible.[16]

Clinical trials offer a particularly clear example of this mechanism, but it is also at work in many other social circumstances. As one example of this, Figure 5.3 can also illustrate the situation of a person who hesitates between investing her money on the stock market or in Government bonds that are safer but have a lower expected yield.

5.4 Mere possibilities

In this section, I will return to uncertainties that are not expressed or even expressible in terms of probabilities.[17] In public debates, it is common to warn against future risks by pointing out that they are possible, without attempting to specify how probable they are. Opponents of biotechnology or nanotechnology want to stop these technologies since they 'can' have disastrous outcomes. Enthusiastic proponents of the same technologies have countered that they must be developed since they 'can' provide cures against deadly diseases, or solve some of the many other problems that plague humanity. I will refer to these as *mere possibility arguments*.[18] A mere possibility argument consists in taking the mere possibility that a course of action will have certain consequences as support for a decision to perform or not to perform that action.[19]

Argumentation based on mere possibilities need not be faulty. In some situations it is quite reasonable to let a mere possibility have a decisive influence on a decision.

> *Example 5.9:*
> On a visit to an arms factory, a person takes up a just finished pistol, puts it against his head and shows intention to pull the trigger, just for the fun of it. Then someone says: 'Don't pull the trigger. You never know, it can be loaded.'

Although there is no good reason to believe that the pistol is loaded, it would seem sensible to heed the warning. However, it is equally easy to find examples in which it is rational to reject a mere possibility argument or consider it overruled. An illustrative such example is offered by the debate on the polywater hypothesis, according to which water could exist in an as yet unknown polymeric form. In 1969, *Nature* printed a letter that warned against producing polywater. The substance might 'grow at the expense of normal water under any conditions found in the environment', thus replacing all natural water on earth and destroying all life on this planet.[20] The author might equally well have mentioned other possible disasters, or brought up the problem of unknown possibilities. Soon afterwards, it was shown that polywater is a non-existent entity. If the warning had been heeded, then no attempts would have been made to replicate the polywater experiments, and we might still not have known that polywater does not exist.[21]

There is no limit to the number of mere possibility arguments that can be created. In a sense, *any* decision may have catastrophic unforeseen consequences. Any new medicine *can* have serious unknown side-effects. Any new industrial chemical *can* become the substrate on which a new bacteria strain develops that gives rise to a devastating pandemic. Any action whatsoever might invoke the wrath of evil spirits (that *might* exist), thus drawing misfortune upon all of us. Clearly, although some mere possibility arguments deserve to be taken seriously, we have no choice but to disregard most of them. A policy to attend seriously to all such arguments would make us hostages to the constructors of fanciful scenarios. We would become victims to superstition, and our general competence as decision-makers would deteriorate.

To avoid this, we need methods for selecting out the consideration-worthy mere possibility arguments. In what follows I will propose such a method in the form of a three-step procedure.[22]

The first step is *disambiguation* of the mere possibility whenever this can be done. By disambiguation is meant that the reference to a mere possibility is replaced by a reference to a more specified degree of possibility. This transformation of the argument makes it easier to come to grips with and facilitates its weighing against other arguments. The following dialogue exemplifies disambiguation:

Angela: 'It would be wise of you to stop smoking. Otherwise the cigarettes can kill you.'

Brian: 'But there are thousands of things that could kill me, and I cannot quit all of them. In the last few months, the newspaper contained articles saying that eggs, meat, milk and I think even more food-stuffs can be deadly. I cannot stop eating all of these.'

Angela: 'There is a big difference. The food-related dangers you mention are all quite uncertain. In contrast, there is overwhelming evidence of the serious health effects of smoking. In fact, scientists have shown that about half of the smokers die prematurely because of smoking.'

Angela opens the conversation by putting forward a mere possibility argument, which Brian tries to neutralize (with a type of argument that we will return to below). Then Angela specifies her argument, thereby transforming it from a mere possibility argument into an argument expressed in probabilistic terms. If she had stopped before the last sentence, her specification would have been non-numerical, but it would still have served the purpose of making the argument more precise and thereby easier to evaluate.

In the assessment of a mere possibility argument, the first step should always be to investigate whether it can be disambiguated in this way. When that is not doable, we proceed to the second step. It consists in applying two *symmetry tests* in order to distinguish specific uncertainty that is potentially decision-relevant from unspecific (or background) uncertainty.

The *test of opposite effects* consists in investigating whether the mere possibility argument can be countered with an argument showing that we have at least as strong reasons to consider the possibility of some other effect that (1) is opposite in value to the effect originally postulated (i.e. positive if the postulated effect is negative, and vice versa), and (2) has equal or larger moral weight than the postulated effect.[23] If such a contravening possibility can be identified, then the mere possibility argument has been defeated.

> *Example 5.10:*
> A breakthrough in genetic engineering has been announced: Ways have been found to control and modify the metabolism of a species of microalgae with unprecedented ease. 'Synthesizing a chemical with this technology is more like programming a computer than modifying an organism,' said one of the researchers. A group of critics demand that the technology be prohibited by international law. They point to its potential dangers, such as the spread of algae that multiply uncontrolled and produce highly toxic substances.

Here, we can apply the test of opposite effects. Arguably, it is equally possible that this technology can be used to solve serious problems that confront mankind. Perhaps modified algae can make desalination cheap enough for large-scale irrigation. Perhaps such algae can be used to produce most of the energy we need with artificial photosynthesis. If this is true, then the prohibition rather than the use of this technology may have dire consequences. This means that the mere possibility argument will be defeated in the test of opposite effects. Of course, this would not settle the issue. After the mere possibility argument has been dispensed with, it remains to carefully consider the other arguments that may bear on the decision.

In the following example, the test of opposite effects does not seem to defeat the original mere possibility argument:

> *Example 5.11:*
> A company applies for an emission permit to discharge its chemical waste into an adjacent, previously unpolluted lake. The waste in question has no known ecotoxic effects. A local environmental group opposes the application, claiming that the substance may have some unknown deleterious effect on organisms in the lake.

It does not seem possible to construct a positive scenario that can counterbalance this negative scenario. We know from experience that chemicals can harm life in a lake, but we have no correspondingly credible reasons to believe that a chemical can improve the ecological situation in a lake. (To the extent that this 'can' happen, it does so with a much weaker 'can' than that of the original mere possibility argument. This difference can be used in a disambiguation that defeats the proposed counterexample.) Therefore, this is a mere possibility argument that resists the test of opposite effects.

The other test, the *test of alternative causes*, consists in investigating whether the mere possibility argument can be defeated by showing that we have at least as strong reasons to consider the possibility that either the same effect or some other effect that is at least as undesirable will come about if the action under consideration is not performed. If this can be shown, then the mere possibility argument has been defeated.

> *Example 5.12*:
> Opponents of nanotechnology claim that its development and implementation will give rise to a 'nano divide', i.e. growing inequalities between those who have and those who lack access to nanotechnology.

An analogous argument can be made for any other new technology with wide application areas. We already have, on the global level, large 'divides' in sanitation technology, food technology, medical technology, communication technology, etc. Under the assumption that other technologies will be developed if we refrain from advancing nanotechnology, other divides will then emerge instead of the nano divide. If this is true, then the nano divide is a non-specific effect that does not pass the test of alternative causes.

In combination, the two tests can disqualify many mere possibility arguments. Those that are left pass on to the third step that consists in the *valuation* of mere possibility arguments according to three criteria: novelty, spatio-temporal unlimitedness, and interference with complex systems.[24]

Beginning with *novelty*, we usually know less about new risk factors than old ones. This can be a good reason to assign more weight to those mere possibility arguments that relate to new phenomena. Hence, it would currently seem reasonable to pay more attention to mere possibility arguments about fusion energy (from which we have no experience) than about fission energy (from which we have experience of about 15,000 reactor years and three serious accidents).

An interesting example of the novelty factor can be found in particle physics. Before new and more powerful particle accelerators have been built, physicists have sometimes feared that the new levels of energy might generate a new phase of matter that accretes every atom of the earth. The decision to regard these and similar fears as groundless has been based on observations showing that these energy levels are no genuine novelties since the earth is already under constant bombardment from outer space of particles with the same or higher energies.[25]

Spatio-temporal limitations reduce the magnitude of potential disasters. The absence of such limitations aggravates uncertainty in many ecological issues. The emission of greenhouse gases is one example of this; another is the spread of chemically stable pesticides that migrate between ecosystems. If a persistent substance diffuses to all ecosystems on Earth, then any deleterious effect that it has may cause irreparable damages.[26]

Finally, *complex systems* such as ecosystems and the atmospheric system are known to have reached some type of balance that may be impossible to restore after a major disturbance.[27] Uncontrolled interference with such systems may have irreversible consequences. The same can be said of uncontrolled interference with economic systems; that is an argument for piecemeal rather than wholesale economic reforms.

The mere possibility arguments that satisfy all three criteria (novelty, spatio-temporal unlimitedness, and interference with a complex system) are the ones that should be assigned the highest weight. However, as always, the weight of an argument must be compared to the weight of its counterarguments. This we can see from Example 5.9. The mere possibility argument in that example, namely that the pistol may for some unknown reason be loaded, does not satisfy any of the three criteria. In spite of this, it has weight enough to provide a sufficient reason not to pull the trigger. This is because of the weakness of the argument in the other direction, the pleasure of playing dare-devil.

5.5 Conclusion

In this chapter we have developed several types of arguments for the moral assessment of situations involving risk and uncertainty. We have introduced three criteria for when expected utility maximization is an appropriate decision rule. We have uncovered the mechanism (uncertainty transduction) by which uncertainty tends to increase the moral leeway. We have also shown how this mechanism operates on uncertainties about probabilities, and clarified how conflicts between two maximization rules (maximization of expectation values and security levels, respectively) can give rise to moral leeway. Finally, we have investigated the relevance of mere possibility arguments and provided a three-step procedure for identifying the more consideration-worthy of these arguments. Each of these rules and procedures applies only to some of the many types of situations in which we need to appraise risk or uncertainty from a moral point of view. There is a need to further develop and systematize the various argument patterns that can be used to deal with different types of situations involving risk and uncertainty.

Part III

Solving Conflicts of Risk

6
Fair Exchanges of Risk

It does not seem possible for a human society to avoid situations in which benefits for some persons lead to risks for others. Therefore conflicts of interest about risk are inescapable. They are also at the centre of many public controversies about risk. To deal with them we need to answer the question: When is it justified to impose a risk on someone else? In this chapter, the outlines of an answer to that question will be presented.

The answer is based on the assumption that we all have a defeasible right not to be exposed to risk by others. This right is introduced in Section 6.1. A preliminary account of the conditions under which it is defeated (cancelled or overridden) is given in Section 6.2, based on the idea of mutually gainful exchanges of risks and benefits. This proposal is fine-tuned in Section 6.3 in order to accommodate requirements of justice and equal influence. Section 6.4 is devoted to a discussion of what is needed to make it work in a democratic decision process.

6.1 A defeasible right

Several principles have been proposed for determining whether a risk imposition is justifiable. Quite a few risk analysts have claimed that there is a general limit between acceptable and non-acceptable risk, usually in the form of a probability limit.[1] The most recent form of this proposal is the 'de minimis' position in risk regulation that postulates a probability threshold, 'a lower bound on acceptable risk levels, no matter what the associated benefits', such as 'a cut-off level of 10^{-6} individual lifetime risk [of death]'.[2] However, it is not difficult to show with examples that even risks with very low probabilities are unjustified if they bring nothing good with them. Even a very small risk imposition needs a justification.[3] (To test the sincerity of a claim that all risks below 10^{-6} are negligible, ask the claimant whether he will let you play 'seven dice Russian roulette' on him. In this game a fair die is rolled seven times in a row. If it lands on a six all seven times, then you play Russian roulette on him with a cartridge in one of the six chambers of the revolver. If he answers yes, then the next question is how many times he will allow the game to be played against him.)

A less unreasonable approach is to weigh the totality of risks that an action gives rise to against its totality of benefits. This is the method implemented in standard risk-benefit analysis. It is based on the plausible assumption that to be acceptable, a disadvantage has to be outweighed by an advantage. It is also based on the less plausible assumption that a disadvantage to one person can always be compensated by a larger advantage to some other person. As we saw in Section 2.2, the resulting disregard for individuals lacks moral credibility. The fact that a certain loss for Ms. Black is smaller than a certain gain for Mr. White does not suffice to make it allowable for Mr. White, or anyone else, to perform an action that leads to this particular combination of a loss for Ms. Black and a gain for Mr. White.[4]

A third approach, the single owner heuristic, is primarily used in legal contexts. Its basic idea is that in negligence cases, 'due care is the care an average, reasonable person takes in his or her *own* person and property.' Therefore, 'the inquiry reduces to whether the average person would take the precaution if he or she bore both the costs and benefits in full.'[5] If applied to risk acceptance, the single owner heuristic would share the problem of the previous approach, namely its programmatic neglect of distributional issues. Suppose that most professional divers would undertake a certain dangerous assignment in exchange for one million dollars. This cannot be used as an argument for an arrangement in which one diver receives the money and another performs the dangerous task. The single owner heuristic does not work for risk imposition problems.

Instead, I propose a fourth approach that has its focus on individual rights. To introduce it, we can use the deterministic case as our starting-point. Everyday moral reasoning does not in general allow gains for one person to cancel out losses for another. I am not allowed to inflict even a minor loss on you against your wish in order to achieve a larger gain for myself or for some third person. This can be expressed as a prima facie rule:

> *The prima facie no-harm principle:*
> Every person has a prima facie moral right not to be exposed to negative impact, such as damage to her health or property, through the actions of others.[6]

The right referred to in this principle has to be defeasible since there are quite a few situations in which it is defeated by other moral principles. Situations when a right of self-defence comes into force are among the clearest examples of this.

The prima facie no-harm principle can be extended from harms to risks of harm. In other words, we should recognize that each individual has a prima facie right not to have risks imposed on her by others.

> *The prima facie no-risk principle:*
> Everyone has a prima facie moral right not to be exposed to risk of negative impact, such as damage to her health or property, through the actions of others.[7]

Just like the no-harm principle, this rule has to be defeasible so that it can yield to other, contextually stronger considerations.[8] There are two major ways to accommodate exceptions in a rule-bound system.[9] According to the *defeasibility* account that has been chosen here, rules do not have an absolute status, and they can therefore be rightly broken when they are defeated by other rules. According to the *exception clause* account, each rule has a complete set of exception clauses built into it. In this way all cases are excluded in which the rule would otherwise seem to be rightly broken.[10] The exception clause account has the advantage that rules may be absolute, but unfortunately it cannot be used for (general) morality due to the complexity and multifariousness of the social situations in which a system of moral rules should be applicable. In order to capture the intricacies of actual moral systems, exception clauses would have to be limitlessly complex. We are not capable of listing in advance all the exceptions (and their exceptions, etc.) that will restrict our applications of a rule such as the no-risk principle.[11] As Alan Goldman has said, 'we cannot predict exceptions generated by genuine novelty.'[12]

Like other prima facie rights, those conferred by the no-risk principle can be defeated in two major ways: they can be cancelled or overridden.[13] When a right is cancelled, it loses all its force. An overridden right, in contrast, may have some force left. The difference can be seen from the following example.

> *Example 6.1:*
> Two years ago, Nadia was approached by a man who introduced himself as her third cousin Ian. Since then they have exchanged quite a few letters and phone calls. Nadia has promised to give him a small silver goblet that is part of her collection of objects made by their great-great-grandfather, who was a renowned silversmith.
> *Case (i):* The day before Ian arrives to pick it up, she finds out that he is an imposter and not at all her third cousin.
> *Case (ii)* The day before he arrives, a thief steals all the other silver articles that she has inherited from her ancestor, leaving only the one that she had stowed away in order to give it to Ian.

In case (i), Ian's moral right to receive the goblet as promised has been cancelled, i.e. it has completely lost its force. In case (ii) it seems to have been overridden, rather than cancelled. Since the goblet is now the only silver article that Nadia has left from her ancestor, it would be unreasonable to require that she gives it up. However, the overridden right has left behind moral residues. Nadia owes Ian excuses and explanations, and if she has a collection of other less valuable heirlooms it would not be unreasonable that she gives him one of these instead.[14]

In practice, the prima facie no-risk principle will have to be overridden in quite a few cases. Otherwise social life would be impossible. When we heat our houses, we emit substances that contribute to the health risks of others. As car-drivers, we put the lives of other road-users at risk. Without these risk impositions we would freeze and be immobile. There are many other, similar examples.[15] We therefore need to identify the overriding considerations in view of which these and similar risk impositions can be accepted in spite of the prima facie no-risk principle. In other words, we need a solution to the following problem:

> *The defeasance problem:*
> Under what conditions is the prima facie no-risk principle defeated (cancelled or overridden), so that someone is allowed to expose another person to risk of harm?

In what follows the justification of risk impositions will be discussed in the terms of rights and defeasance that have been introduced in this section. However, this choice of a terminology does not commit us to a full-blown rights-based ethics.[16] Rights can also be accommodated in a broadly based consequentialist system, or in some other moral framework, some but not all of whose ethical building-blocks are rights.

6.2 Reciprocal risk impositions

When searching for a solution to the defeasance problem, our task is not to develop a special theory for a small fraction of social issues, the 'risk issues'. Risk is pervasive in both private and social decision-making. Almost all social decisions involve strivings to avoid undesirable future events that may or may not take place.[17] Therefore, issues of risk neither can nor should be isolated from other social issues. We need methods to include risk-related moral considerations in our general decision-making processes.

As a background, two potential but not very promising solutions to the defeasance problem should be mentioned:

(1) Exposure of a person to a risk is acceptable if this exposure is outweighed by a greater benefit.
(2) Exposure of a person to a risk is acceptable if this exposure is outweighed by a greater benefit for that person herself.

Rule (1), or at least the idea behind it, was already rejected in Section 2.2 for the simple reason that it focuses exclusively on aggregate values and offers no protection of individual rights. Rule (2) goes very far in the opposite direction. We can see this from the traffic example mentioned above. It is of no use to me that people whom I do not know are allowed to drive their private cars in my home-town, but their car driving increases the risk that I will be the victim of a traffic accident or some disease related to air pollution. They, on their side, have no use for me driving a car. In short, we have incentives to disallow each other's car driving. Hence, the implementation of rule (2) could expectedly stop all motor traffic – and in the same way it could put an end to a large proportion of the other technological activities that take place in a complex society. This rule would probably make human society impossible.

We need to find a compromise between the extreme permissiveness of (1) and the extreme rigidity of (2). Such a compromise can be obtained by extending a simple principle that we all apply individually: Each of us takes risks in order to obtain benefits for ourselves. This exchange of risks and benefits can be extended to exchanges between individuals that are beneficial to all of them. If others are allowed to drive a car, exposing me to certain risks, then in exchange I am allowed to drive a car and expose them to the corresponding risks. With such reciprocal exchanges of risks and benefits, we can all lead more mobile lives. Presumably, this is on balance beneficial to all of us.[18] As a first approximation, we can express this solution to the defeasance problem as follows:

(3) Exposure of a person to a risk is acceptable if this exposure is *either* outweighed by a greater benefit for that person herself, *or* part of a social practice in which other persons are exposed to the same risk, and the benefits to her from this practice outweigh the risk.

This rule has the important advantage of recognizing each person's individual rights, while still making mutually beneficial adjustments possible (contrary to the more simplistic rights-based approach to risk that was discussed in Section 2.4). It does not allow you to stop your neighbour from driving a car, even though her driving imposes a (small) risk on you as a pedestrian. Instead, it allows both you and her to use this method of transportation, which is presumptively beneficial to both of you. On the other hand, rule (3) would prohibit exploitative arrangements in which someone is exposed to risks in order to achieve benefits only for others.

However, in an important sense, rule (3) is still too restrictive: It only allows for agreements in which two or several persons accept *the same* risk in exchange for some benefit. Exchanges of different risks are not covered; in other words, rule (3) allows us to exchange apples for apples, but not apples for pears. In order to reap the advantages of modern society with its division of labour and its complex production of commodities, we also need to engage in exchanges of different types of risks and benefits.

This can be seen from the following example: A factory in your neighbourhood manufactures product *A*, which you do not use. The factory emits a chemical substance that gives rise to a very small risk to your health. At the same time, another factory, far away from your home, emits other chemicals in the production of product *B* that you use. One of the neighbours of this second factory does not use product *B*, but instead uses product *A*. In this way, and sometimes in much more complex chains, we may be said to exchange risks and benefits with each other.

There is an obvious moral limit to such arrangements: Their total effects should be to the benefit of all concerned. No single person should be exposed to risks to an extent or in ways that cannot be justified by benefits to herself, either directly or indirectly through risk exchanges with others. We cannot require that every single risk-exposure be to the risk-exposed person's benefit, but the totality of risk-exposures should be so arranged that everyone gains, and no one is exploited. This is expressed in the following rule:

(4) Exposure of a person to a risk is acceptable if this exposure is part of a social practice of risk-taking that works to her own advantage.

The first disjunct in rule (3) is left out in rule (4). For practical purposes we can assume that if a risk-exposure is beneficial to a particular person, then it is subsumable under a social practice of risk-taking that works to that person's advantage. With this interpretation, rule (4) allows everything that rule (3) allows, and more in addition to that.

The reference in rule (4) to a social practice allows us to make decisions on groups or types of risk-exposures rather than separately on each particular risk-exposure.[19] We can have general rules such as those permitting automobile traffic (under conditions such as traffic rules) and those prohibiting the use of certain pesticides and authorizing the use of others (under conditions such as compliance with specified safety instructions).[20] It would be impracticable to make a separate assessment of each new instance of a potentially risk-creating activity.

Ultimately, the social practice mentioned in rule (4) can refer to the whole society. In principle, risks in widely divergent social areas can be parts of one and the same social exchange. You may be more risk-exposed than me on your workplace, whereas I am more exposed to health risks from pollution in the ambient air or from the locally produced food that I eat. In practice, however, it is impossible to keep track of the combined distributional effects of risk exchanges across different social sectors and make sure that compensation takes place whenever necessary. Therefore, the risk exchanges referred to in rule (4) should primarily concern risks and benefits within the same social sector, such as the sectors of transportation, industrial production, healthcare, etc.[21]

Under the assumption that there is a practice of mutually beneficial exchanges of risk-taking in a specific social sector, such as that of transportation, is that practice binding on everyone? It would be difficult to maintain that it is binding for a person who never uses it, such as someone who lives in an isolated community that does not use modern means of transportation.[22] One the other hand, someone who uses the services that are based on it (in this case: modern transportation) can be considered as de facto accepting it. We can therefore restrict rule (4) to those persons who do not seclude themselves from the social practice we are considering:

(5) Exposure of a person to a risk is acceptable if this exposure is part of a social practice of risk-taking that works to her own advantage and which she de facto accepts by making use of its advantages.

It is instructive to compare rule (5) to rule (1), which is the dominating approach in risk analysis. By choosing a rule such as (5) rather than (1), we transform the agenda for discussions on risk. We choose to treat each risk-exposed person as a sovereign individual with a right to fair treatment, rather than treating her as a carrier of utilities and disutilities whose values would be the same if they were carried by someone else. According to rule (1) and to traditional risk analysis, in order to show that it is acceptable to impose a risk on Ms. Smith, the risk-imposer only has to give sufficient reasons for accepting the risk as such, as an impersonal entity. According to the present proposal, this is not enough. The risk-imposer has to give sufficient reasons why Ms. Smith – as the particular person that she is – may be exposed to the risk. This cannot be done credibly by referring to aggregated, impersonal benefits. It can, however, be done by showing that this risk-exposure is part of an arrangement that works to her own advantage.

But rule (5) is not our final solution to the defeasance problem. There are still some difficulties to resolve. In particular, rule (5) is too permissive in two respects, i.e. it approves of two types of risk exchanges that a more plausible principle should exclude. The first of these are risk exchanges that are unfair although they are to everyone's advantage, for instance exchanges that are immensely beneficial to some individuals but only marginally beneficial to others. The other type is risk exchanges that have been decided over the heads of the risk-exposed. As citizens in democratic societies, we expect to be rulers of our individual lives and to have a say in the collective issues that concern us. Hence, rule (5) has to be adjusted to include requirements of justice and influence. These adjustments are the topics of the next section.

6.3 Justice and equal influence

Consider a hypothetical society whose labour force is divided into two classes. The higher class leads a protected life, whereas the members of the lower class have dangerous occupations, live in unhealthy buildings, and can only afford unwholesome food. For the higher class, this system appears to be a most advantageous arrangement.[23] For the lower class, it is only marginally better than living outside of society. Such an arrangement should be excluded by a fully adequate rule for risk exchanges, but it appears to be compatible with our rule (5). To exclude it, we have to amend the rule and require that an individual who is exposed to a risk receives a fair share of the advantages that her risk-taking contributes to making available to society.

The relevance of justice to the justification of risk-taking is borne out by practical experience. In current societies, people who are underprivileged in other respects also tend to be more risk-exposed.[24] For most of these differences, no morally tenable justification seems to be available.

What more precisely does it mean for a distribution of risks to satisfy the requirements of justice? A traditional answer to that question would specify what a perfectly just distribution of risks should look like. But for our present purposes this is not the most useful way to answer the question. The introduction of a requirement of perfect justice into rule (5) would make the amended rule impracticable. Few if any mutually gainful risk exchanges would be allowable if all such exchanges were conditional on a perfectly just social system for risk-taking. On the other hand, it is not an unrealistic demand that the social system for risk-taking should strive efficiently in the direction of justice. This requirement also has the advantage of avoiding some of the problems that arise when we try to specify perfect justice. It is no easy task to define what a perfectly just social distribution of risks should be. It is much easier to identify the direction and the immediate tasks of strivings for justice.[25] The obvious targets of reform are the high risk-exposures of people who are also disadvantaged in other social and economic respects.

Two additional specifications should be made of the concept of justice. First, we are concerned with individual justice, as distinct from justice between families or other groups of people. At first, this may seem to be a trivial qualification. Ideologically, we have since long given up the idea that justice requires 'visiting the iniquity of the fathers upon the children unto the third and fourth generation'.[26] Presumably, almost no one would accept today that a person is punished or otherwise legally disadvantaged for what their parents or ancestors have done or been subjected to. However, as soon as we leave criminal justice and consider broader social justice, we will find widespread acceptance of arrangements by which children are severely disadvantaged due to the misdeeds or misfortunes of their parents. At the time of writing, one of the major political controversies in the United States concerns whether children of poor families should be subject to the increased health risks that are associated with lack of a health insurance.[27] In all countries, it is in practice accepted that differences in home and family conditions give rise to large differences in the life chances and life risks of children. We still let children suffer from the shortcomings and misfortunes of their parents.

Today it is uncommon to find an explicit defence in moral terms of why the failings of parents should befall their children. It is difficult to see how a credible argumentation to that effect could be constructed.[28] (In actual social and political debates, these differences tend to be treated as immutable background conditions, rather than as changeable social conditions for which explicit argumentation is needed.) As we have already noted, rule (5) differs from rule (1) in treating each risk-imposed person as a sovereign individual with a right to fair treatment. The introduction of a requirement of justice into the rule should not reverse that improvement. Therefore, the justice requirement should refer to individual justice.

The other specification concerns whether social measures that aim at justice should be taken repeatedly or on a single occasion only. Proponents of the latter view claim that justice is achieved if everyone has the same starting line. 'Thus, if a number of people start out with equal shares of material resources, and fair opportunities (whatever exactly that may mean), other things being equal, there seems to be no basis for objecting to the justice of the outcomes of any voluntary exchange we might make.'[29]

A starting line theory can be either transgenerational or individual. In a transgenerational starting line theory, the equal starting line may be far back in history. According to an individual starting line theory, it is the starting line of each individual that counts. Suppose that your and my ancestors lived under the same conditions at some point in history. Mine were clever and rose to a privileged position, whereas yours gradually sank to the lowest social stratum. Then I will start my life with much better preconditions than you. According to an individual starting line theory, this would be unfair, but according to a transgenerational starting line theory, you would have no morally valid reason for complaint. (The best-known transgenerational starting line theory was put forward in Robert Nozick's *Anarchy, State and Utopia*, but was later retracted by its author.[30]) Since transgenerational starting line theories punish us for the failures and the bad luck of our ancestors, they are not compatible with the individual conception of justice that we have already chosen. An additional problem with such theories is of course their lack of historical realism. We have no reason to believe that there ever was a period in human history when everyone had equal conditions, and from which all future changes have developed through morally acceptable moves.[31]

The starting line theories that remain for consideration are therefore the individual ones, according to which we should all start out from equal starting lines, in terms of educational opportunities and other resources in childhood and adolescence. To achieve this ideal, radical changes would be needed in any existing society. Nevertheless, the principle of equal starting lines does not include everything that social justice requires. The only credible reason why equal starting lines should be sufficient seems to be the assumption that if we are provided with the same initial conditions, then any differences that follow will depend on our own actions and choices, and for these we can be held accountable.[32] This assumption might have been true in a deterministic world, but it is far from true in the world that we live in.[33] Our living conditions are not determined exclusively by our starting lines and our own actions. To the contrary, our lives are pervaded by risk and uncertainty, and no one is in more than partial control of her own life. A person can run into difficulties due to an unexpected dismissal of personnel from the company where she works, a serious disease affecting herself or a member of her family, or a host of other such factors that she had no chance even to foresee.[34] Therefore, starting line justice is insufficient, and we need to apply principles of justice to events in life later than a starting line in childhood or adolescence.[35] There is also another, more pragmatic reason to do this: Even if starting positions can be evened out to a considerable extent, this cannot be done perfectly, and injustices will remain. Compensatory policies later in life can to some extent indemnify for failures to fully equalize starting lines.

In conclusion, when we adjust rule (5) to incorporate considerations of justice, the amended version should refer to *individual* justice, and its individuality should be taken seriously. This means that if someone has poor life chances and big life risks, then it is no excuse that this depends on the (possibly culpable) failures of her parents or ancestors. Furthermore, since injustices arise throughout our lives due to events beyond our control, justice is not achievable by setting the initial conditions right and then leaving the system to its own. Justice should be a strong, continuous counter-force to the various social mechanisms that unceasingly tend to perpetuate, accumulate, and reinforce injustices. This is summarized in the following amendment of the principle:

(6) Exposure of a person to a risk is acceptable if this exposure is part of a persistently justice-seeking social practice of risk-taking that works to her advantage and which she de facto accepts by making use of its advantages.

In spite of being an improvement over our previous candidates, rule (6) still suffers from a serious problem: it does not require that the risk-imposed have any influence over the risk. We could, at least in principle, imagine that a well-meaning dictator distributed risk impositions among his subjects in full accordance with rule (6). Such a system would be unacceptable since it does not respect the risk-exposed individual as an autonomous person who should be in control of her own life. We expect to make our own decisions in our private lives. We also expect to have a say and a vote in the issues that affect so many people besides ourselves that the decisions have to be public rather than private.

However, there is a limit to how much influence each of us can have over the risks that we are exposed to, without endangering the social benefits from activities that involve risk-exposures. Letting everyone have maximal influence would be tantamount to giving all of us a veto, so that all risk decisions depend on consensus among the risk-exposed.[36] For reasons we have already discussed, this would lead to a society of stalemates in which it would be extremely difficult to move forward in any direction. Therefore, we all gain from limiting the individual influence so that we can make mutually gainful risk exchanges. This means that instead of maximal influence *tout court*, we should settle for the maximal influence that all individuals can have while still reaping the advantages of social co-operation (in the form of risk exchanges). For that purpose, an additional clause should be added to rule (6):

(7) Exposure of a person to a risk is acceptable if (i) this exposure is part of a persistently justice-seeking social practice of risk-taking that works to her advantage and which she de facto accepts by making use of its advantages, and (ii) she has as much influence over her risk-exposure as every similarly risk-exposed person can have without loss of the social benefits that justify the risk-exposure.

This is our final approximation of a solution to the defeasance problem. Clause (i) is the condition of *fair risk exchange* and clause (ii) that of *maximal equal influence*.[37]

6.4 Conclusion

With rule (7) we have arrived at a solution to the defeasance problem presented in Section 6.1. With this solution, we can eschew the disrespect for individual rights and interests that characterizes standard risk analysis, while at the same time allowing socially gainful risk-taking to take place. However, like other rules for social decision-making, rule (7) requires a certain amount of agreement in order to function appropriately. In particular, a practice of risk exchanges presumes at least approximate agreement among those concerned about how serious a risk is and how valuable its associated benefits are. Perfect agreement on the values of risks and benefits is not required, but large differences are bound to generate tensions that are difficult to resolve. Suppose that someone proposes that, in exchange for some social benefits, we should all accept some risk that she considers to be minimal. Furthermore, suppose that you and many others differ from the proposer in considering this risk to be huge. It will not be easy to reach an agreement under such conditions. The same applies if there are large differences in the valuation of benefits. The differences in how we value fast transportation contribute to explaining many controversies on road traffic and the risks that it gives rise to. Differences in appraisals of nuclear energy and genetically modified organisms have sometimes been large enough to make these issues almost impossible to deal with even in otherwise well-functioning democracies.

There is no simple solution to this problem, but there is a basic insight that is necessary for dealing with it in a democratic society: Democracy is not only a formal system for counting votes and electing representatives. The democratic idea also includes the ethos of democracy, without which a democratic system is unworkable. It is an essential part of the democratic ethos that the participants should be willing to make compromises and that they should prefer decisions by large rather than small majorities.[38] If we act according to the democratic ethos, then we should do our utmost to avoid decisions by a majority of barely above 50 per cent in issues that are crucial for social coexistence. It is characteristic of well-functioning democracies that the major political actors aim at consensus in issues that set the stage for social co-operation, such as foreign policies and constitutional reform. This is something that we have learnt gradually from our experience of democracy. The need for consensus was not well understood by early proponents of popular rule. (For Robespierre it was no problem to make a majority decision to oppress a minority.[39]) Even today, lack of democratic ethos is often a major problem in new democracies.

Decision-making on risk has often been impeded by insufficient understanding of the democratic ethos and what it requires. Too often it has been seen as unproblematic if a majority decides to introduce a technology that a large minority sees as a risk of doomsday proportions. There is also a tendency to move risk issues from the political arena to expert committees whose members lack the mandate and the experience necessary to deal with policy issues that require negotiated solutions. Many issues of risk are so conflict-ridden and so fundamental to human coexistence that they should, to the contrary, be treated in the way that constitutional issues are treated in most democracies. This means that although the decision ultimately has to be made by a majority, that majority must first engage in a serious dialogue with the concerned minorities. All participants in such a dialogue have a democratic obligation to attempt seriously to reach, through mutual adjustments, a decision that everyone can live with.

7
Moral Excuses under Scrutiny

In the previous chapter a procedure was proposed for determining when it is ethically defensible to expose another person to a risk. We are now going to consider three types of arguments that can be seen as attempts to bypass such a discussion by presenting an overriding reason why a risk imposition should be accepted.

First, we have cases when the effects of a risk imposition are impossible to observe. A toxic exposure can increase the probability of a disease by a small number that cannot be statistically distinguished from no increase at all. Risks that are too small to be detected are usually taken to be of no concern. In Section 7.1 we will discuss whether undetectability is a sufficient justification for risk impositions.

Secondly, there are cases when the risk-exposed person has consented to the exposure. Consent is a standard requirement for medical treatment, and appeals to its justificatory force are also common in other social areas. It is not difficult to find examples where consent renders a risk imposition acceptable that would otherwise have been unacceptable. But does it always make a risk imposition justifiable? That is the topic of Section 7.2.

The third and final category consists of acts that contribute to a risk that the exposed person also contributes to herself. Typical examples are selling cigarettes to a smoker and heroin to an addict. Many such acts are taken to be morally unproblematic. In Section 7.3 we will investigate the moral status of such contributory acts of risk imposition. In Section 7.4 some concluding reflections will be offered on the nature of the moral investigations that we have performed.

7.1 Undetectable effects

Modern societies are willing to pay much higher sums of money to save known individuals than individuals whose identity cannot be determined. Trapped miners and patients in need of expensive life-saving treatments are examples of the former. In contrast, most measures undertaken in preventive medicine 'only' save statistical lives. Consider a campaign against smoking among young adults. About half of those who abstain from smoking due to this programme will live longer lives than what they would have done otherwise.[1] However, it is impossible to identify those who would otherwise have died prematurely. The programme does not save any identified persons, only 'statistical' persons. Such programmes tend to receive much less funding per saved life than measures that save identified persons. This has been called the discrimination of statistical victims.[2]

It does not seem to have been seriously proposed that such statistical effects are matters of no concern. However, there is a related category of risks that have often been treated as unproblematic, namely risks that are undetectable even by statistical means.[3] The following somewhat oversimplified example will clarify the distinction:[4]

Example 7.1:
There are three substances *A*, *B*, and *C*, and 1000 persons exposed to each of them. Exposure to *A* gives rise to hepatic angiosarcoma among 0.5 per cent of the exposed. Among unexposed individuals, the frequency of this disease is very close to 0. Therefore, the individual victims can be identified.

Exposure to *B* raises the incidence of leukaemia from 1.0 to 1.5 per cent. The number of victims will be the same as for *A*. However, although we know that about 10 of the about 15 leukaemia patients would also have contracted the disease in the absence of exposure to the substance, we cannot find out who these ten patients are. The connection between substance *B* and leukaemia is detectable only on the collective, not on the individual level.[5]

Exposure to *C* leads to a rise in the incidence of lung cancer from 10.0 to 10.5 per cent. Just as in the previous case, individual victims cannot be identified. In addition, since the difference between 10.0 and 10.5 per cent is indistinguishable from random variations, the effects of this substance are undetectable not only on the individual but also on the collective level.[6]

As this example shows, undetectable effects may be fairly large, judging by the standards we apply to risks in a human population. As a rough rule of thumb, epidemiological studies cannot reliably detect excess relative risks that are about 10 per cent or smaller. For the more common causes of death, such as lung cancer and ischæmic heart disease, lifetime risks are between 1 and 10 per cent. Therefore, even in the most sensitive studies, excess lifetime risks of such major diseases cannot be detected if they are in the magnitude 10^{-2} to 10^{-3} or smaller.[7] In public policy, a risk of this size, i.e. between 1 in 100 and 1 in 1000, is usually considered to be a major concern.[8]

A possible objection should be dealt with at this point: If a risk is undetectable, then presumably we cannot know that it exists. If this is so, then undetectable risks would seem to be practically irrelevant, since we cannot identify and act against a risk as long as it belongs to that category.

But this is not so. Even if an effect is undetectable, we may know, or at least have strong reasons to believe, that it exists. By 'detection' of a phenomenon is meant that its existence is ascertained through a reasonably direct empirical observation or measurement. A phenomenon may be undetectable even though there are convincing theoretical reasons to believe that it exists. If we add a small amount of hot water to a lake, the effect on the lake's temperature may be completely undetectable. Whatever difference in temperature we can measure is indistinguishable from random variations. But we know from elementary physics that our action has raised the temperature of the lake. This effect is knowable in spite of being undetectable. In the case of toxic substances, reasonably reliable information is often obtainable from animal data that can be combined with background knowledge on toxic mechanisms to provide strong evidence that a substance causes toxic effects in humans.[9]

In public debates it is often claimed that if an exposure has taken place without any harmful effects being detected, then there is nothing to worry about. Most of these statements are made by laypersons, but sometimes similar claims are made by professed experts or by authorities with access to expertise. In 1950 Robert Stone, a radiation expert with the American military, proposed that humans be exposed experimentally to up to 150 roentgens (a dose that can give rise to acute radiation sickness) with the motivation that 'it seems unlikely that any particular person would realize that any damage had been done on him by such exposure'.[10] Another unusually clear example is a statement by a former chairman of the American Conference of Governmental Industrial Hygienists (ACGIH), a private standard-setting body with a strong influence on occupational exposure limits throughout the world.[11] He conceded that the organization's exposure limits 'can never be used to guarantee absolute safety', but found it sufficient that 'they can be used to control adverse health effects of all types below the point at which they cannot be distinguished from their background occurrence'.[12] In a documentation report on vinyl chloride, a substance known to cause occupational cancer, the ACGIH's standard-setting committee wrote:

> 'A TLV–TWA [threshold limit value – time weighted average] exposure concentration of 5 ppm [parts per million] is recommended. It is the judgment of the TLV Committee that, if the average airborne exposure concentration to vinyl chloride does not exceed 5 ppm, there should be no detectable increase in the incidence of occupational cancers, specifically angiosarcoma of the liver.'[13]

Similarly, the Health Physics Society wrote in 1996 in a position statement on radiological protection:

> '... [E]stimate of risk should be limited to individuals receiving a dose of 5 rem in one year or a lifetime dose of 10 rem in addition to natural background. Below these doses, risk estimates should not be used; expressions of risk should only be qualitative emphasizing the inability to detect any increased health detriment (i.e., zero health effects is the most likely outcome).' [14]

The underlying assumption in these and similar pronouncements is that if a potential risk factor does not give rise to any detectable detrimental effect then it does not give rise to any risk of concern. In other words, it is assumed that undetectability is in itself a sufficient justification for risk impositions. The implications of this assumption can be seen from the following hypothetical example:

> *Example 7.2:*
> There are three forms of lung cancer in the general population, called variants I, II, and III. Variant I has the frequency 10 per cent in the general population, and variant II the frequency 1 per cent. The frequency of variant III is close to zero. The three variants have the same clinical symptoms, the same treatment, and the same prognosis. The difference is inconsequential for the individual patient, and can only be detected through laboratory tests.

> Substance *A* was previously used by a large plastics manufacturer. It gave rise to lung cancer of variant III among 0.5 per cent of the exposed workers. This effect was clearly detectable on the individual level. Some of the affected workers were interviewed in the media on their deathbeds. These interviews gave rise to considerable public relations problems for the company.
>
> Then the company came up with a replacement, substance *B*. Just like its predecessor, it gives rise to lung cancer among 0.5 per cent of the exposed workers, but in this case the cancer is of variant II. Therefore, the effect was now undetectable on the individual level. However, it was still detectable on the collective level. A few years after the substitution, epidemiological evidence was published, showing that the incidence of work-related cancer had not diminished, only shifted type.[15] This gave rise to a public uproar against the company.
>
> In the meantime, the company had continued its research, and it could therefore respond swiftly to the public criticism by replacing *B* with the new substance *C*. Like its two predecessors, the new substance gives rise to lung cancer among 0.5 per cent of the exposed, but in this case the cancer is of variant I. Therefore, the effect is no longer detectable even on the collective level. Finally the company has solved its public relations problem.

Has the company also solved its moral problem? The answer should be obvious as soon as the moral problem is correctly identified. The moral problem is that the company's workplace conditions give rise to cancer among its employees. The moral problem is *not* that it is *known* that the company's workplace conditions give rise to cancer among its employees. (If that were the problem, then we could solve many public health problems by prohibiting epidemiological studies and barring physicians from asking patients about environmental and occupational exposures.) Clearly, the replacements of *A* by *B*, and *B* by *C*, did not solve the moral problem.

We can conclude from all this that undetectability is not the all-round justification of risk impositions that it has often been taken to be. However, it does not follow that (individual or collective) detectability has no relevance whatsoever in a moral appraisal of risk. A plausible argument for its relevance can be based on the special obligations that we owe to certain people. I have, for instance, special duties to my children. My duty to come to their assistance is greater than my corresponding duties to my neighbour's children. Similarly, my duties towards the neighbour's children, with whom I am reasonably well acquainted, seem to be stronger than those towards complete strangers. A special weight emanates from the relationships that we have developed with individuals who have come our way. As was noted by John Cottingham, such personal bonds are 'an unavoidable part of what it is to be a human being. To say that the moral outlook is one which should attempt to ignore or transcend these bonds is to propose a concept of morality which seems inconsistent with our very humanity.'[16]

It does not seem unreasonable to extend this special weight, but in a weakened form, to fellow human beings with whom we could form personal relationships, even though we have not done so.[17] This could then explain why we can have stronger obligations towards identified victims such as trapped miners than towards statistical victims. In other words, we can give trapped miners higher priority than the statistical beneficiaries of preventive medicine for the same type of reason that we give higher priority to our kin and friends than to (identified) strangers.

A public official is under a special duty to be impartial.[18] This is the reason why we have procedures such as recusal (judicial disqualification) to protect public decisions from the influence of private relationships. However, the problems of partiality in public office do not seem to affect the weaker form of human relationship that extends to all identifiable fellow human beings. Therefore, this justification for special obligations to identifiable persons can be applied to public policy as well, and it will then strengthen our moral obligations to identified persons at risk. However, the absence of such personal relationships is not sufficient to justify risk impositions. The conclusion stands: That which we cannot detect may nevertheless be morally indefensible.

7.2 Consent

Consent is one of the most common arguments in favour of risk impositions. If it can be shown that the persons at risk consent to the exposure, then it is often assumed that the argument ends there. This standpoint has been particularly clearly expressed in the context of occupational risks.[19] Similarly, risks associated with consumer products and leisure activities are often defended with reference to the consent of the consumers. This approach was expressed and defended by McCarthy under the rubric of the Consent Idea: 'if an agent has the right that others not bring about p, then it is permissible for others to bring about p if the agent consents'.[20]

There can be no doubt that consent is morally relevant in many if not most situations with risk impositions.[21] Exposing someone to a risk tends to be morally worse if that person objects to the exposure than if she consents to it. This is not what is at stake here. Instead the question is whether consent is such a strong argument that it is in itself sufficient to justify a risk imposition.

The notion of consent as it is used in contexts of risk has its origins in medical ethics. In the second half of the 20th century, medical ethics was transformed from an older paternalistic tradition to a new way of thinking with a strong emphasis on patient autonomy and self-determination. In the new medical ethics, informed consent has become a central concept.[22] It serves to ensure that no other medical procedures are performed on the patient than those that she has chosen herself.[23] Many attempts have been made to extend the application of informed consent to other settings than healthcare.[24] It is in these extensions, rather than in medical contexts, that consent has been taken to be sufficient to justify risk impositions. In medical ethics, consent is standardly considered to be a necessary but insufficient condition to legitimize an intervention. Administering a treatment that does more harm than good to the patient's health is considered to be unethical, however much the patient consents.[25] There are also striking differences between the criteria of voluntariness for consent in different domains.[26] In healthcare, consent must be obtained without any pressure or enticement such as payment. This is of course very different from the notion of consent that is referred to when a worker who accepts employment is said to thereby consent to the risks at the workplace.

Although we usually speak about consenting to a risk, this is a somewhat misleading terminology since people seldom consent to a risk *per se*. It cannot be enough emphasized that risk-taking does not in general consist in choosing free-floating risks but rather in choosing combinations or 'packages' of risks and benefits. A person who consents to the risks of a surgical operation does this because of the advantages associated with the operation. She would not consent to the risks alone. (That would be approximated by an operation in which she is anesthetized and the surgeon performs all the risk-inducing parts of the surgery, such as cutting through adjacent tissues, but not the part that has therapeutic effects, such as removing the sick tissue.[27])

An example adopted from Judith Thomson illustrates the point.[28] A woman decides to take a short-cut through a dark park at night although she knows that crimes are common in that park. In doing so she takes a risk, and some may even want to say that in a way she consents to the risk. Now suppose that she proposes to the county council that they make the park safer, for instance, by lighting or police patrolling. It would seem rather outlandish if they dismissed this proposal with the argument that she and other night-wanderers have already consented to the risk by entering the park. It would be even more absurd if, after an assault, the perpetrator maintained that she had no reason for complaint since she had consented to the risk of an assault.

What is wrong here is of course the assumption that she consented to the risk of assault *per se*. What she did was to choose the package consisting of this risk and the benefit of a shorter route (and perhaps some badly needed fresh air). She chose this package since there was no other package available that would give her the same benefit(s) without the associated disadvantage of a risk of assault. She would presumably not consent to some other alternative that increased her risk of being assaulted equally much, but without the associated benefit. (This would be approximated by taking a route through a disreputable dark street with the same increased risk but no time gain, fresh air, or other advantage.) Therefore, it would be wrong to say that she consented to being assaulted or even to the risk of being assaulted. What she chose (and in a sense consented to) was a package of time-gain *cum* risk of assault. It is fully consistent for a person who makes this choice to also be highly critical of the prevailing social situation in which the benefit in question (the time-gain) is unavailable without the associated risk of assault.

Next, consider a worker who accepts a job with a high risk of serious injury, such as working in a mine with unusually many rock falls. Presumably, he would not accept this risk alone; he would not be the least attracted by the prospect of spending eight hours a day in the mine without being paid for it. What he has accepted is the package consisting of these risks and the benefits associated with the job, such as the pay and perhaps the comradeship and the opportunity to stay in the community where he was born. If there were an alternative job open for him with the same advantages but much lower accident risks, then he would presumably not work in the dangerous mine. Among the packages available to him he has chosen this one. His choice can be described as an expression of consent, but it is neither consent to the risk *per se* nor to the construction of the package that he chose. His standpoint is fully compatible with being a trade union activist who demands safety improvements on the workplace.

For a final example, consider a person who chooses to bungee jump. It would be compatible with common usage to say that in making this choice she consents to the risks associated with the jump. However, what she consents to, as should now be clear, is not the risk *per se* but a package consisting of this risk and its associated advantages. The advantage sought is the thrill, not the risk of dying or being seriously injured. If she had the choice of an otherwise exactly similar jump but with a safer cord, then she would presumably choose the safer alternative.

Hence, what we usually call consent to a risk is in fact nothing else than the choice of a package consisting of this risk and some advantages that cannot be obtained without it. Once this has been understood, it should be clear that such consent cannot in general serve as a sufficient justification for risk impositions. The county council cannot legitimately dismiss demands to make the park safer at night with the argument that those who choose to walk there have thereby consented to the risks. Their choice of the available package of park-walking and assault risk does not imply that they consent to the county council's decision not to offer instead a package in which park-walking at night is much safer. This argument extends to the examples of workplace safety and bungee-jumping. That a person makes a choice under circumstances that she cannot influence does not mean that she consents to these circumstances.

It could be argued against all this that there are situations when someone looks for a risk *per se*, and not as a means to obtain some associated benefit. Clearly there are cases of self-destructive behaviour, but for several reasons they have only limited relevance for social risk-taking or risk imposition. Self-destructive behaviour often emanates from curable psychiatric conditions. Even more importantly, self-destructive behaviour usually takes the form of actively harming oneself, rather than taking dangerous jobs or consenting to other forms of risk impositions. People who go through dark parks, take dangerous jobs, or bungee jump have not chosen to harm themselves. Therefore the argument 'but they have a right to harm themselves' is not relevant in cases like these. A person's right to harm herself in certain ways does not justify a decision to offer her certain advantages only in combination with risks of such harms.

Furthermore, the concept of consent has a fundamental limitation that makes it unsuitable as an all-round justification of risk impositions: It does not signify full participation in a decision but only influence in the final stage when the options have been selected and what remains is to choose between them.[29] To exemplify this, consider the case of a rich investor who orders an investigation of several investment alternatives, carefully studies the experts' advice and then authorizes them to implement one of these alternatives. It would be strange to say that he has given consent to how his money is invested. He has agreed (consented), but he has also done much more, namely had a decisive influence over the whole decision-making process. The term 'consent' would be more appropriate in the case of a small saver who authorizes a bank official to do as the latter proposes.

This limitation in consent can also be seen in the paradigmatic medical examples. The potential research subject in a medical experiment does not take part in the development of the experimental procedure. She only decides whether or not to be a subject in an experiment developed by others. Similarly, a patient giving consent to a treatment makes a choice between the therapeutic options proposed by medical professionals. In these cases, the restriction does not seem to be inappropriate. It would not be realistic for patients to take part in the preliminary discussions in which the treatment alternatives are developed. But as we have already seen, the restriction is much more problematic in many non-medical cases.

It is no coincidence that the term 'consent' is used more often in risk issues than in most other policy areas. The consent perspective expresses a low level of ambition with respect to public participation that is typical of much risk policy. 'Consent' tends to be a catchword in policies that are less concerned with involving citizens in the full decision process than with obtaining a *carte blanche* from the public for projects and proposals developed by an élite. (Other linguistic signs of the same tendency are the frequent use of the term 'acceptance' in relation to risk and the focus on the public's trust in decision-makers rather than their democratic control over the decision-makers.) Here is an unusually clear expression of that sentiment, as expressed in a scholarly article:

> 'Community groups have in recent years successfully used zoning and other local regulations, as well as physical opposition (e.g., in the form of sitdowns or sabotage), to stall or defeat locally unacceptable land uses. In the face of such resistance, it is desirable (and sometimes even necessary) to draw forth the consent of such groups to proposed land uses.'[30]

If a person is given the choice between alternatives that have been constructed or selected for her by others, then her choice in that situation of one of these alternatives – be it 'drawn forth' or obtained in a more complaisant way – cannot be taken as proof that she prefers it to the options that were excluded from her choice. This is the basic reason why a person's consent to a risk (as consent is usually understood) is not in general a sufficient moral justification for exposing her to that risk.

7.3 Contributions to self-harm

In most situations when someone is exposed to a risk, actions and decisions by several persons have contributed to the risk-exposure, directly or indirectly. Typically, some but not all of these actions were performed by the risk-exposed person her- or himself. When a worker is injured through a machine failure, the causal factors include the worker's own decision to take a job with potentially dangerous machines, the employer's or his representative's decision to buy the machine in question, their further decisions about its use and maintenance, the machine manufacturer's decisions about its construction, etc. Similarly, behind a smoker's death from a smoking-related disease there is a complex combination of causes, including the smoker's decision (many years ago) to smoke her first cigarette, but also many decisions by cigarette manufacturers and others who contribute to the tobacco epidemic. It is in fact difficult to find a clear example of a risk-exposure that does not have, among its causal factors, both actions by the risk-exposed and actions by others.[31]

As we saw in Section 3.3, when several causal factors contribute to an event, a choice to call one of these 'the cause' is not dictated by the nature of things. In practice, such choices depend to a high degree on social conventions. From a moral point of view, it is particularly important whether 'the cause' is selected among the actions of the risk-exposed person or among other actions or events. In the case of smoking, the conventional view holds forth the smoker's own contribution. Smoking is described as a life-style risk, and by implication smoking-related diseases are regarded as self-inflicted. However, there are also cases when the risk-exposed person's own contribution is not treated as 'the cause'. Even if Susan's careless way of carrying her handbag was the reason why the bag snatcher chose her as a victim, we refer to the thief's rather than Susan's action as the cause of her losing the bag. Almost any victim of a crime could have taken more precautions, but we tend to assign causality to the acts of the perpetrator rather than to those of the victim.[32] (However, this is not a rule without exceptions, as many rape victims have experienced.)

As these examples show, assignments of causality have important implications for how we morally assess the actions of the risk-exposed person. In addition, causality assignments are equally important for the moral assessment of actions by others than the risk-exposed who contribute to the risk. If actions by the risk-imposed persons are among the causal factors, and in particular if 'the cause' is found among these factors, then this is often used as a moral excuse for others who contributed to the risk.

Smoking is a clear example. As we just noted, the smoker who is harmed by her smoking has herself made some of the decisions that contributed to the condition. Tobacco companies use this as a moral excuse for themselves. In doing so, they take it for granted that the smoker's responsibility for the outcome pre-empts any responsibility on the part of others who contributed to it. This is often expressed in the form of a professed opposition to paternalism. Tobacco companies have sponsored anti-paternalist campaigns that focus on the right of smokers to smoke.[33] The assumption is that if it is paternalist to interfere with the smoker's right to smoke, then it is also paternalist to interfere with the sale and marketing of tobacco products.

Paternalism consists in interfering with someone for her own good. It is important to note that paternalism comes with a benevolence condition: An action can only be paternalist if it is performed for the good of the person in question.[34] This terminological condition gives rise to a strange asymmetry in some discussions on paternalism. Imposing on a person the burden of wearing a bicycle helmet is paternalism, but imposing the burden of breathing unhealthy air is not – for the simple reason that the first but not the second imposition is for her own individual good. Some critics of meddlesome politics seem to be much more worried about the former (paternalistic) form of interference in people's lives than about the latter.

But let us have a closer look at the pro-tobacco argument just referred to. Although it is described as an anti-paternalist argument, it is not, for the simple reason that the actions that it protects are not self-harming. A company that sells tobacco and promotes its use does not thereby harm itself or its owners. It harms other people, namely the smokers whom it recruits and sustains. Therefore, this argumentation amounts to an extension of antipaternalism so that it also protects certain acts that harm others. Such *extended antipaternalism* should be distinguished from antipaternalism proper that refers to non-interference with self-harming actions and activities.[35]

Once the distinction has been made between antipaternalism proper and extended antipaternalism, it becomes clear that no general inference from the former to the latter is possible.[36] We may well approve of Mill's dictum that the only reason to interfere with someone's behaviour is to protect others from harm, without accepting the marketing of tobacco or heroin, boxing promotion, driving with unbelted passengers, buying sex, or other actions that contribute to a harm that the harmed person also contributes to herself. A person's moral right to expose herself to a risk or a harm does not necessarily imply a right for others to facilitate or contribute to her doing so. Hence, although many would claim that we all have a right to kill ourselves with cyanide, few would maintain that this implies a moral right to sell and promote the use of convenient suicide doses of cyanide.

Clearly, a risk-exposed person's contribution to a risk often diminishes the moral blameworthiness of others who contribute to the same risk. Selling poison to an acutely depressed person who uses it in an attempted suicide is (ceteris paribus) not as blameworthy as sneaking it into her food, but it may nevertheless be blameworthy to a considerable degree. The same argument applies to other actions that contribute to risk exposures, such as selling dangerous products to people, hiring them for dangerous jobs, etc.

The ways in which we in practice distribute responsibilities in cases with mixed causality largely result from social conventions rather than from consistently applied moral principles. This can be clearly seen from differences in responsibility ascriptions between cases that are structurally similar. The manufacture and sale of tobacco is conventionally protected by the moral excuse that smokers are themselves responsible for their habit. In contrast, the corresponding argument for heroin is seldom taken seriously. (Cigarettes are legal and heroin illegal, but that does not settle the moral issue.) In moral philosophy, such conventions should not be treated as self-evident background conditions. Instead they should be highlighted and, when appropriate, called into question and challenged by alternative views.

A hypothetical example can further clarify how our appraisals of responsibility depend on social conventions. Suppose that a major soft drink company comes up with a new product that customers will become addicted to. The new soft drink has no serious immediate health effects, but in the long run it will give rise to pulmonary, cardiovascular, and various malignant diseases, thereby ultimately shortening the lives of about half of the consumers who become addicted to it. Few would claim that the sale of such a product should be allowed. Yet, its properties are analogous to those of cigarettes.[37] The difference is of course that cigarettes are socially accepted and that it is considered politically impossible to prohibit them.

Boxing provides another instructive example.[38] Discussions on professional boxing are typically couched in terms that would have been adequate if the two combatants were standing together in the ring, each punching on his own face rather than that of his opponent. A more realistic analysis of boxing will have to recognize at least three types of responsibility-conferring actions. First, each boxer performs the self-harming action of letting the other hit him. Secondly, each boxer performs the (reciprocal) other-harming action of hitting his opponent. Thirdly, managers and promoters perform the (one-sided) other-harming action of inducing the boxers to hit each other. In the parallel examples of duels, street fights, and unauthorized prizefights, the corresponding other-harming actions are considered to confer responsibility for resulting bodily injuries (in spite of the concomitant and causally necessary self-harming action). Again, the difference is one of social convention, not consistently applied moral principles. These conventions developed before modern knowledge about the brain damage induced by boxing, just as the conventions concerning cigarette manufacture and sale developed before modern knowledge about the health effects of smoking.

These are only a few of the many causality- and responsibility-ascribing conventions that determine our social policies of risk. Some of these conventions may be 'hidden' in the sense of being so entrenched in our thinking and taken so much for granted that we do not easily see them. The disclosure of such assumptions is an important task for ethics-based social criticism. One of the aspects that should then be scrutinized is the extent to which inordinate blame is placed on the victims of harmful social practices, thereby averting attention from potential targets of social reform. [39]

As an example of this, the conventional view on traffic accidents puts a strong emphasis on the responsibility of individual drivers. Suppose that a driver drives too fast, loses control over the vehicle and hits another vehicle so badly that several persons are killed. Such an accident is considered to be caused by the speeding driver, and the responsibility will be assigned to him or her, not least in the legal aftermath of the accident. However, there are many other causal factors at work in this case. Society has decided to build roads that allow for high velocities. Automobile manufacturers have decided to sell cars that can be driven at much higher velocities than the maximum allowable speed. Governments have chosen to allow the sale of such cars. An interesting comparison can be made with other types of dangerous machines. A punch press can cut off a worker's fingers unless provided with a safety switch that stops the press if an object approaches the dangerous zone. Machines without such a protective device are prohibited in most industrialized countries. A car is an even more dangerous machine. The proneness of drivers to speed is no less prominent than that of machine workers to put their hands into a punch press. Furthermore, whereas the punch press would 'only' cut off the fingers of the operator, driving at excessive speed often harms and kills other people. (This makes a mechanical implementation of the speed limit less paternalistic than the safety switch.) Under the assumption that speed limits are taken equally seriously as other life-saving laws and regulations, it is not easy to justify the sale of vehicles that can be driven at a much higher speed than what is allowed on any public road.

7.4 Conclusion and outlook

We have investigated three types of arguments that are often used as moral excuses for risk impositions:

The effect is undetectable.

The affected persons have consented.

The affected persons have themselves contributed to the risk.

We have seen that none of these is sufficient to justify a risk imposition. Instead, the more stringent requirements on such justifications that were outlined in the previous chapter will have to be applied.

This book has focused on one particular aspect of ethical theory, namely its ability to account for risk and uncertainty. I will conclude with some more general reflections on the development of ethical theory. Moral philosophy consists primarily in systematic reflections on how we humans should act in our relations to each other. Our actions do not take place in a vacuum but in a natural and social environment. Since this environment is constantly changing, so is the subject matter of moral philosophy. Developments in human society constantly provide moral philosophy with both new issues and new perspectives on old ones. This is perhaps most clearly seen in retrospect. There is a long list of developments in the previous century that had a deep influence on moral philosophy: the emergence of democracy, the holocaust, the threat of a nuclear war, feminism, destruction of the environment, neurobiology, biotechnology, etc. Currently, new issues are in need of thorough ethical discussions, including climate change, new medical technologies, and new forms of terrorism.

Therefore, the task of moral philosophers is not to produce timeless and contextless ethics – we might just as well run after the end of the rainbow – but to develop moral theory in relation to our changing society.[40] Such an endeavour does not seem to be well served by the assumption that moral inquiry consists in discovering a pre-existing and unique, 'true' moral theory. This is a standpoint with many adherents – from utilitarians to religious fundamentalists. It is in my view not only unfounded but also socially dangerous since it stands in the way of the democratic and open-ended process that is needed to develop a common set of basic values in a society.

It has sometimes been claimed that unless we believe that there is a uniquely correct moral theory, we cannot take morality seriously. This is a misconception of what it means to take something seriously.[41] Whether you believe something to be objectively given and whether you believe it to be important are two distinct questions. One can hold one's moral views to be worth fighting for without believing them to have an objective ground in the order of things.

Notes

Introduction

1. Moore [1912] 1958, p. 118 (ch. V); Waddington 1960, p. 18; Coyne 1985, p. 324.
2. Moral philosophy is affected by at least two major types of uncertainty: uncertainty with respect to facts and with respect to moral values. This book focuses on the former type (but the latter is briefly discussed in Section 1.3). On uncertainty about values, see Lockhart (2000).
3. In his *New Essays on Human Understanding* (1704), Leibniz complained that moralists had an inadequate and too limited view of probability (Leibniz [1704] 1962, p. 372 (IV:2,§14); English translation in Leibniz [1704] 1996, p. 372). – Cf. Teuber (1990, p. 236).
4. The idealization used in most of moral theory is in fact much stronger than determinism. The consequences of alternative actions are assumed to be not only determined but also knowable at the point in time of deliberation. For reasons of convenience, the term 'deterministic' is used here to denote such conditions for (moral) decision-making.
5. Hardin (1989, p. 69).
6. Rosebury (1995, esp. pp. 499 and 505). On the use of unrealistic examples in philosophy, see also: Quine 1972, p. 290; Lucey 1976; Lackey 1976; Abbott 1978, pp. 318–319; Levi 1987; Ward 1995; Hansson 2006c and 2006f; Fried 2012.
7. Hansson (2006h).
8. Hansson (2001b and 2010b).
9. Hansson (2009b). Here and in what follows, I use 'moral appraisal' as a unifying term that covers both moral evaluation and moral prescription, i.e. statements about both values and norms.

1 The Uncertainties We Face

1. Hansson 2005b and 2007e.
2. In this it differs from 'benefit'. Therefore, the term 'risk-benefit analysis' (unintendedly) signals asymmetrical comparisons. It would be more symmetric to weigh risks against chances or benefits against harms.
3. Hansson 2002b.
4. Fischhoff et al. (1981, p. 2) defined risk as the existence of a threat to life or health. In this sense of 'risk', the word 'hazard' is often a useful synonym (Hansson 2009d).
5. Van de Vate and Kelly (1978, p. 118) claimed that 'risks ought to be minimized; to be minimized, they must first be quantified.' This is wrong.

Minimization can be based on a binary relation, cf. Hansson (1989b). On the usefulness of a binary representation in this context, see Hansson (2012a).

6. Due to differences in sensitivity, this probability may be different for different persons who are exposed to the same physical conditions (Hansson, 2009e).
7. Royal Society 1983, p. 22; Graham and Wiener 1995, p. 30; Kress 1995, p. 282; Edwards 2005, p. 255. In the same vein, the US National Research Council (1983) defined risk assessment as an assessment of the 'probability that an adverse effect may occur as a result of some human activity'.
8. This idea can be found from the beginning of probability theory. In the Port Royal Logic we read: 'Puis donc que la crainte d'un mal doit être proportionnée non seulement à la grandeur du mal, mais aussi à la probabilité de l'évenement, comme il n'y a gueres de genre de mort plus rare que de mourir par le tonnerre, il n'y en a gueres aussi qui nous dût causer moins de crainte, vû même que cette crainte ne sert de rien pour nous le faire éviter' (Arnauld and Nicole [1662] 1965, p. 354). ('Since the fear of an evil ought to be proportionate not only to the magnitude of the evil but also to the probability of occurrence and since there is scarcely any kind of death rarer than death by thunder, there is hardly anything that ought to occasion less fear – especially since that fear does nothing to avoid such a death' (Arnauld [1662] 1964, p. 356).
9. Bondi 1985, p. 9.
10. Cohen 1985, p. 1.
11. Cohen 2003, p. 909.
12. Biwer and Butler 1999, p. 1158.
13. Rechard 1999, p. 776. Expected utility theory was introduced by Daniel Bernoulli (1738). His text has been interpreted as an account of risk in terms of expected utility, but the text does not support this interpretation. Bernoulli speaks of 'mensura sortis', the measurement of a lot (a share decided by lot). In the English translation (Bernoulli [1738] 1954), this is misleadingly rendered as 'measurement of risk'. – The definition of risk as expected utility appeared in economic literature before it was used in risk analysis, see for instance Domar and Musgrave (1944). (I am grateful to Margarida Lima Rego who brought this paper to my attention.)
14. The International Organization for Standardization (2002) defines risk somewhat vaguely as 'the combination of the probability of an event and its consequences', where 'combination' is often (but need not be) interpreted as multiplication.
15. Hansson 2006e.
16. The Royal Society (1983, p. 23) proposed the term 'detriment' to denote the integrated product of risk and harm. This proposal has not received much following.
17. Klemm 1989.
18. Hansson 2010a.
19. Charnley 1999 and 2000. On the notion of objectivity, see Douglas (2004). In the traditional expectation value account of risk, subjectivity can affect both the probability and the utility.
20. Wynne 1992.
21. Hansson 2007d and 2012b.

22. The distinction between risk and uncertainty is usually attributed to Frank Knight ([1921] 1935) and J.M. Keynes (1921), but it was already present in the work of J. H. von Thünen (1783–1850) (Reddy 1996). For an overview of early 20th century work on uncertainty, see Arrow (1951).
23. Luce and Raiffa 1957, p. 13.
24. See Section 1.1.
25. Hansson 1999d and 2010d.
26. It would have been much more clarifying to distinguish between decisions under 'probabilized uncertainty' (risk) and 'unprobabilized uncertainty' (uncertainty), but the prospects for a terminological reform seem meagre.
27. Differences between objective frequencies and estimates (for instance by experts) of such frequencies are well-known from experimental psychology, where such differences are described as lack of calibration (Hynes and Vanmarcke 1976; Christensen-Szalanski and Bushyhead 1981; Lichtenstein et al. 1982; Griffin and Brenner 2004; Budescu and Johnson 2011).
28. Hansson 2009c. On the inadequacy of the gambling metaphor, see also Price (1999, p. 272).
29. Hansson and Johannesson 1997; Hansson 2006d.
30. Jeffrey 1956.
31. Hansson 1996b and 2003c.
32. Bengtsson 2006; Ross and Matthews 2009.
33. The constructors of the first nuclear bomb were concerned with the possibility that the bomb might trigger an uncontrolled reaction that would propagate throughout the whole atmosphere (Oppenheimer 1980, p. 227).
34. Hansson 2007b.
35. Hansson 1996a.
36. Hansson 2010c.
37. Savage 1972, p. 83; Bordley and Hazen 1992.
38. Hansson 2010b.
39. Spohn 1977; Rabinowicz 2002.
40. These examples are taken from Hansson (2007b).
41. The money already paid for the 12 months membership is a so-called sunk cost. In traditional microeconomics, it is considered irrational to allow such costs to influence a decision (the 'sunk cost fallacy'). However, in some cases it may be rational to take sunk costs into account (O'Brien and Folta 2009).
42. Adler and Stewart 2009; Banja 2004.
43. http://www.dn.se/insidan/insidan-hem/svenskarna-bast-i-varlden-pa-riktigt-langa-aktenskap. Downloaded January 26, 2013.

2 Difficulties for Moral Theories

1. Hansson 2007f. It is not always an advantage to have ready-made answers to all moral questions that may arise: see Hansson (2012c).
2. For a virtue ethical approach to risk, see Athanassoulis and Ross (2010). For a discourse ethical approach, see Pontzen (2007). For an overview of the ethical literature on risk impositions, see Hayenhjelm and Wolff (2012).
3. It is a debated issue whether a risk imposition is in itself a harm or whether there is no harm unless the risk materializes. See for instance Perry 2007;

Finkelstein 2003; Kumar 2003; and Oberdiek 2009 and 2012. As was noted by Steigleder (2013), this is a terminological question with no action-guiding implications. Exposing someone else to a danger can be morally reprehensible even if she is not harmed. On distinctions in moral theory that have no action-guiding implications, see Hansson (2013a).

4. Another type of mixture problem arises when one person's action is one of several contributing causes of an outcome. See Sections 3.4 and 7.3.
5. Hansson 1991 and 2001a, pp. 143–144.
6. We can assume that the potential objects of normative appraisal form a subset of the set of potential objects of value judgments. Hansson 2001a, p. 129.
7. Cf. Klibanoff 2001.
8. See Sections 3.1 and 3.2.
9. Hansson 1993.
10. Sen 1979 and 1999, pp. 58–60.
11. Hamlin 1989, p. 174.
12. Hansson 2004c.
13. Zimmerman (2008, pp. 38–42) uses the term 'expectable value' to denote expected value in cases when the value function is derivable as a probability-weighted aggregation of several value functions, representing value uncertainty. The problems for utilitarian expected utility maximization discussed below apply to that variant as well.
14. Carlson 1995, pp. 119–144; Garvin 1953, pp. 231–247; Singer 1977 and 1982; Lomasky 1978; Jackson and Pargetter 1986; Vallentyne 1987; Strasser 1989; Carlson 2002; Zimmerman 2008, pp. 119–127. – An early debate on actualism took place between Moore ([1912] 1958) and Russell (1966, pp. 13–59). See also Broad ([1914] 1971).
15. Singer 1977 and 1982.
16. Jackson and Pargetter 1986, p. 233.
17. Cf. Thomson 1986, p. 185; Bradley 2005; and Zimmerman 2006.
18. Moore ([1912] 1958), pp. 118–120.
19. According to J.J.C. Smart, a prominent defender of actualist utilitarianism, 'act-utilitarianism is meant to give a method of deciding what to do in those cases in which we do indeed decide what to do' (Smart and Williams 1973, p. 44).
20. Schoemaker (1982, p. 529) rightly noted that expected utility maximization is 'the major paradigm in decision making since the Second World War', and similarly Anand (1993, p. 131) said: 'There can be few theories that would appear to be so important in so many disciplines.' Utility calculations are performed in PRA and in CBA, but they are seldom performed in philosophy. Donagan (1977, p. 203) observed concerning utilitarian philosophers that 'what ought to astonish readers of their work is neither the complexity nor the difficulty of utilitarian calculations, but their absence.'
21. Hansson 1993; Feldman 2006, p. 56.
22. Critics have maintained that serious events with low probabilities should be given a higher weight in decision-making than what they receive in the expected utility model (O'Riordan and Cameron 1994; O'Riordan et al. 2001; Burgos and Defeo 2004).

23. On possible evolutionary advantages of risk aversion, see Okasha (2007 and 2011). See also Section 5.1.
24. In this respect, risk analysis stands in sharp contrast to mainstream economic science in which reallocations without mutual consent are usually seen as problematic (Hansson 2004a and 2006d).
25. Hansson 1993, p. 24. A similar example is discussed in Reibetanz (1998, pp. 302–303).
26. Other rules from decision theory, such as the maximin rule and the minimax regret rule, are equally problematic. On the maximin rule, see Section 2.5. On the minimax regret rule, see Hansson (1997b).
27. Parfit 1997.
28. Leonard and Zeckhauser 1986.
29. The term 'deontological' is sometimes interpreted more broadly as referring to non-consequentialist moral theories in general, but the more restricted sense will be adhered to here. – In ordinary language, the terms 'duty' and 'obligation' differ in meaning, as explained in Brandt (1965). Here they will be treated as synonymously expressing what may be called the common core of the prescriptive words. Cf. Hansson 1988a and 2001a, pp. 131–133.
30. This interdefinability was referred to already in the twelfth century (Knuutila 1981, pp. 236 ff). See also von Wright (1951 and 1968, p. 3).
31. The word 'concerning' is chosen since the duties may be duties either to perform or not to perform the actions in question.
32. This was called the 'problem of paralysis' by Hayenhjelm and Wolff (2012). See also Broome, 1978.
33. Cf. Hardin 1989, p. 70.
34. Hansson 1988a; 2001a, pp. 137–138; and 2013b. Thanks are due to Peter Vallentyne for proposing the term 'obligation assessment'. In previous work I use the term 'veritable obligation'.
35. Conflicts can also arise from the combination of three or more obligations although no conflict arises between any two of them. Cf. the definitions of obeyable predicates in Hansson (1999b and 2001a, p. 167). Furthermore, conflicts can arise between two or several permissions. Suppose that I have said to each of my two neighbours: 'When I am on vacation, you can use my lawn-mower at any time you want'. Then a conflict can arise if the two neighbours want to use it at the same time.
36. Frankena 1952, p. 194.
37. Coval and Smith 1982, p. 455; Nickel 1982, p. 257; Kamm 1985, pp. 121–122; Hansson 1988b.
38. Marcus 1980, p. 135. Cf. Morton 1991, p. 48.
39. Hansson 1998b.
40. The typology of rights referred to here was presented in Hansson (1996c and 2001a, pp. 208–222).
41. This refers to the central legal relation of the right. A right is a legal complex that also includes various subsidiary moral relations including, in this case, the obligations of legal officials to implement such a will. On the distinction between the central and the subsidiary legal relations associated with a right, see Wellman (1975, pp. 52–55) and Hansson (2001a, p. 215).

42. A third, practically somewhat less important category is the revocable permissions, i.e. permissions that one person has unless someone else revokes it. See Hansson (2001a, pp. 217–218).
43. Nozick 1974, p. 7. Cf. McKerlie (1986) and Sobel (2012).
44. Rights concerning actions can be of four different types. If a person *A* has a right, then this can be (1) a right for *A* to perform some action, (2) a right for *A* not to perform some action, (3) a right for *A* that some other person *B* performs some action, or (4) a right for *A* that some other person *B* does not perform some action.
45. For simplicity, Probabilistic absolutism is formulated here for only one of the several forms of rights, namely a right that someone else does not perform a specified (type of) action. In order to show that Probabilistic absolutism does not work for rights in general, it is sufficient to show that it is unworkable in this case. The same applies to the Probability limit approach that is discussed below.
46. Cf. Fried 1978, pp. 18–20; Schroeder 1986, pp. 526–527; Kagan 1989, p. 88; and Lübbe 1998, p. 186.
47. Nozick 1974, p. 75.
48. Railton (1983) and McKerlie (1986) reached negative conclusions on the capacity of traditional rights theories to deal with risk impositions. For a somewhat more positive view, see Rogerson (1984, p. 119).
49. The idea of a social contract was used in the late 16th century by opponents of absolute monarchy, in particular in the Huguenot movement. In pamphlets such as the anonymous *Vindiciae contra Tyrannos* (1579) monarchy was claimed to be based on a contract with the people that is invalidated if the King does not fulfil its conditions (Barker 1930; Höpfl and Thompson 1979). In contrast, Thomas Hobbes in his *Leviathan* (1651) invoked the social contract to justify absolute monarchy. The major difference is that he conceived the contract between king and people as absolutely binding for the people, also in subsequent generations.
50. Gauthier 1986; Scanlon 1998.
51. Given the interdefinability of prohibition and obligation (see note 30) it would make no difference to replace prohibition by obligation in this definition.
52. Fotion 1987; Hansson 2006b.
53. *Oxford English Dictionary*, online version, accessed in January 2013.
54. An indirect contract-theoretic justification of majority decisions is possible; the participants in the contract may all agree to forthwith acquiesce in majority decisions.
55. Dworkin 1975. The use of hypothetical consent is part of a general trend in ethics that was described by R.M. Hare (1973a, p. 149) as 'hypothetical choice theories'. By this is meant theories, such as hypothetical contract theories and ideal observer theories, in which the right answer to moral questions is the answer that a person or group of persons would choose if placed under certain conditions. If these conditions are strong enough to 'deductively determine the choice' (ibid.), then the ethical problem appears to be reduced to a decision-theoretical problem. (Of course, ethical values have not been eliminated but only focused on the construction of the hypothetical

conditions for choice (Cf. Hansson 2010b.) – For a defence of the view that hypothetical consent can give rise to obligations, see Stark (2000).

56. Altham 1983, pp. 21–23.
57. Rawls 1972, p. 137. Cf. Rawls 2001, pp. 14–18.
58. Rawls's original phrase was 'least advantaged representative man'. (Rawls 1972, p. 151) Given his endorsement of gender equality (Rawls 2001, pp. 64–66), the phrase 'least advantaged representative person' seems more appropriate.
59. The same applies to Gauthier's (1986) Archimedean point, defined as the position an individual must occupy in order for her decisions to have sufficient moral force (p. 233). The ideal actor who occupies that position should be unable to identify herself as a particular person within society, but there are no limits on her knowledge about the society and its members (pp. 235–236).
60. Harsanyi (1953, 1955 and 1975) assumed that the individuals in the original position have an equal chance of becoming any of the actual individuals. In defence of his own proposal, Rawls (2001, p. 106) pointed out that decision-making in the original position takes place under uncertainty rather than risk, since there is no basis for probability assignments. See Kolm (1998) for a comment on this discussion. See also Hare's (1973b) critical discussion of Rawls's maximin solution and Howe and Roemer's (1981) defence of it in game-theoretical terms.
61. A contractarian approach to risks is defended in Nida-Rümelin et al. (2012). Some aspects of contract theory are incorporated into the account of permissible risk impositions in Chapter 6.

3 Back to Basics

1. Kant's moral philosophy is often taken as the epitome of non-consequentialism. Nevertheless, consequences have an important role in his ethics, as can be seen from his 'Über ein vermeintes Recht aus Menschenliebe zu lügen' (On a supposed right to lie from philanthropy) (Kant [1797] 1912). If you cause a harm by telling the truth, e.g. answering truthfully the assassin's question about the victim's whereabouts, then according to Kant you do not 'strictly speaking, *do* the harm to the one who suffers by it; instead, an accident *causes* the harm' (p. 428). However, if you tell a lie, then you are 'responsible for its consequences even before a civil court and must pay the penalty for them, however unforeseen they may have been' (p. 427). This would apply for instance if your lie induces the assassin to go somewhere else, and the victim unexpectedly turns up in that place and is killed (English translations from Kant, 1996, pp. 613–614).
2. Kupperman 1980, p. 325.
3. Sosa 1993, p. 112.
4. Sen 2000, p. 489. See also Sen (1983); Skorupski (1995); Scanlon (1998, pp. 88–90); and Louise (2004).
5. Sen 2000, p. 491; Kupperman 1980, p. 329.
6. Spielthenner 2005, p. 219.
7. For an overview, see Carlson (1995, pp. 10–13 and 48–70).

8. This categorization is essentially taken from Spielthenner (2005); see esp. pp. 223–224.
9. von Wright 1963, p. 116.
10. von Wright (1963, p. 116) used the term 'result' to denote the total state of affairs that contains all the direct consequences. Spielthenner (2005) used 'result' about a single direct consequence.
11. As this example (from Ross 1941) may remind the reader, the relationship between the moral status of a causal effect and that of its logical consequences has been extensively debated in deontic logic. Cf. Hansson 2001a, pp. 141–143; 2006a; and 2013b.
12. Sosa (1993, p. 112) used the term 'analytical consequences' and Brink (1986, p. 420) the term 'conceptual consequences' for this wider category of direct consequences.
13. Bennett (1995, p. 39) called them 'non-causal consequences'. Zamir (2001, p. 158) used the term 'effect' in a wide sense that includes them.
14. For a simple formal model, let a be an action under a particular description and let $ç(a)$ be the set of sentences representing its causal effects. (On the description-dependence of causal effects, see Spielthenner 2005, p. 230.) Let Cn be a consequence relation (Hansson 1999e, pp. 25–31). Then the direct consequences of a under the description in question are $\mathrm{Cn}(ç(a))$. The combined consequences can be written $\mathrm{Cn}(ç(a) \cap f(a))$, where f is a function that selects (sentences representing) the contingent facts that can be combined with $ç(a)$ to form consequences. – These definitions are simple at the price of being, intuitively speaking, too inclusive. Since tautologies are logical consequences of anything, any tautology will be an element of $\mathrm{Cn}(ç(a))$ for any a. Furthermore, that which must be the case irrespective of whether the act is performed or not will be counted as a consequence of the action. Hence, it was a consequence of Jacob Johan Anckarström's act of killing the king of Sweden in 1792 that Sweden was at that time a monarchy. These problems can be solved with a more elaborate definition, such as one that identifies the direct consequences of a with $\mathrm{Cn}(ç(a)) \setminus \cap_{x \in A} \mathrm{Cn}(ç(x))$, where A is the set of alternatives to a (Cf. Gibbard and Harper 1988).
15. In the formal notation, the breadth of consequences is encoded in the function f.
16. According to Amartya Sen (2000, p. 484), it would be arbitrary to exclude a priori any particular component.
17. Let a denote my act of lighting the match, x that the match burnt, and y that the house burnt. Since both x and y are true, so is the sentence $x \leftrightarrow y$ saying that x and y are equivalent. Therefore, if f is unrestricted, then $x \leftrightarrow y \in f(a)$. Since $x \in ç(a)$ we then have $y \in \mathrm{Cn}(ç(a) \cup f(a))$.
18. Sen 1983 and 2000; Louise 2004; Portmore 2007.
19. Sosa 1993, pp. 101–102. See also: Kupperman 1980, p. 325; Pettit 1988; Zamir 2001.
20. Altham 1983, p. 23.
21. Hermansson and Hansson 2007.
22. Hansson 2013a.
23. Thomson 1984, p. 110; and 1986, p. 176.
24. In standard decision theory, no distinction is made between an alternative and its closest deterministic analogue.

25. Pattanaik and Xu 1990 and 2000; Sugden 2003; van Hees 2004; Gustafsson 2010.
26. I.e., both on *ç*(*a*) and *f*(*a*).
27. Mill [1843] 1996, pp. 327–334. (*A System of Logic*, Book III, Chapter V, Section 3.)
28. In Mackie's (1974) terminology, the background conditions form the causal field against which the explicit causal explanation is developed.
29. Hoover 1990, p. 217. Cf. Hesslow 1981.
30. Rizzi and Pedersen 1992; Mosley 2004. – As a further complication, assignment of causal status is not always independent of moral assessment, or conceptually prior to it. Even if a woman's outgoing behaviour was the factor that led the rapist to choose her rather than someone else as a victim, most of us would consider it outrageous to claim that her behaviour caused the crime. Cf. Section 7.3.
31. Russell 1913, p. 1.
32. Russell 1913, p. 14.
33. '...les mouvements d'une horloge, ou autre automate, de celle de ses contrepoids et de ses roués.' (Descartes [1632] 1987). – On Boyle's mechanistic views, see Chalmers (1993), Anstey (2002), Pyle (2002), and Chalmers (2002).
34. Kuhn 1971.
35. Hausman and Woodward (1999, p. 565); Healey (1994).
36. Dent 2003.
37. Berger 1998, p. 324.
38. This applies not only to consequentialists. A critic of consequentialism wrote: 'Apart from a Day of Reckoning, causal chains do not simply come to an end. Our short-term actions sometimes have long-term or long-distance effects, so to measure the consequences of our actions, we need to specify a finish line...' (Guay 2005, p. 350). See also note 41.
39. Hesslow 1981; Lee 1988; Kvart 1991. For an attempt to save transitivity, see Hall (2000).
40. It is of course also possible to operate with two distinct notions of causality for different purposes.
41. See for instance Vallentyne (1987, p. 58); Sosa (1993, p. 106); and Zamir (2001, p. 156). Several critics of utilitarianism have taken it for granted that chains of cause-effect relationships can be followed indefinitely into the future, and see this as a problem for utilitarianism. See for instance Lenman (2000, p. 350); Guay (2005); and Simons (1999, p. 58n).
42. There is considerable controversy over the use of causal concepts in historical studies. See Ringer (1989).
43. Kupperman 1980, 321–322.
44. Prior (1956, p. 94) arrived at a similar conclusion on the ground that it is 'quite impossible to draw a sharp line and say that everything on one side is a consequence of the action; and everything on the other side a consequence of other things; and therefore impossible to arrive at a set of total consequences of the action'.
45. Hansson 2010b. Cf. also the discussion of the so-called lawn-crossing problem, see Harrison (1953, p. 107) and Österberg (1989).
46. Kernohan 2000.

4 Reflecting on the Future

1. According to Thomas Aquinas, prudence consists in the ability to deliberate well with respect to some goal ('bene posse consiliari... in ordine ad finem aliquem', Aquinas 1966, p. 197), and he specifically mentioned that prudence can serve moral goals. (p. 209) He also emphasized that prudence consists in knowing the future from the past and the present (p. 194). On Hobbes' view on prudence, see Vanden Houten (2002). A clear statement of the view of prudence as egoistic can be found in Sidgwick, according to whom 'Prudence may be said to be merely Wisdom made more definite by the acceptance of Self-interest as its sole ultimate end.' (Sidgwick [1907] 1962, p. 328) Mulvaney (1992, p. 444) proposed that we 'reappropriate the venerable word' and remove the 'egoistic connotations' that it has in modern English. Trebilcot (1974) defined the 'principle of prudence' as referring to the maximization of intrinsic value, and compatible with both egoistic and non-egoistic views of intrinsic value.
2. A comparison with John Rawls's contractarian theory can clarify the intended function of this proposal. The two major components of Rawls's theory are a framework for reasoning (the original position) and a set of criteria (primarily his 'two principles of justice') that can be used to evaluate alternative courses of action from the viewpoint of moral or political philosophy. Rawls himself emphasized the independence of the two components and noted that '[o]ne may accept the first part of the theory (or some variant thereof), but not the other, and conversely'. (Rawls, 1972, p. 15) The intended function of hypothetical retrospection corresponds to that of the first of these two parts of Rawls's theory.
3. Mo Tzu 1963, pp. 39–49.
4. Chan 1963, p. 44 (*Analects* 15.23).
5. Matthew 7:12, King James' Bible.
6. An-Nawawi, *Forty Hadith*, number 13. See also Wattles (1996).
7. Parfit 1984. Cf. Singer 1982, pp. 381–382.
8. I use the noun 'alternative' to denote an option that can be chosen in a particular decision. A 'branch' (or 'branch of possible future development') is one of the possible developments after a particular event (typically after the choice of an alternative). For the present purposes, a branch is not followed indefinitely into the future but only to a certain point in time that, in combination with the branch itself, constitutes a 'viewpoint' from which evaluations can be made. (Cf. Section 3.4.)
9. The idea of hypothetical retrospection is an extension and regimentation of patterns of thought that are prevalent in everyday moral reasoning. Unsurprisingly, numerous instances of related ideas can be found in the philosophical literature. Careful consideration of one's future interests was recommended by Plato's Socrates in *Protagoras*. (Prot. 356a-e). In classical accounts of prudence, the moral perspective from future hindsight was a key component (Mulvaney 1992; Vanden Houten 2002). Sidgwick stated that 'a man's future good on the whole is what he would now desire and seek on the whole if the consequences of all the different lines of conduct open to him were accurately foreseen and adequately realized in imagination at the present point of time.' (Sidgwick [1907] 1962, pp. 111–112) However, the

branches ('lines of conduct') that he referred to were under the control of the agent and did not refer to risk or uncertainty. John Rawls's notion of a rational plan of life includes a requirement that 'a rational individual is always to act so that he need never blame himself no matter how things finally transpire.' (Rawls 1972, p. 422; for comments see Williams 1976, and Ladmore 1999.) Nagel (1970, pp. 57–76, esp. 71–72) proposed a principle of temporal neutrality for practical judgments. Nagel's ideas have been interpreted by Donna Dickenson (1991, p. 51) as a remorse-avoiding strategy. In decision theory, regret-avoiding strategies have been given exact formal interpretations (Bell 1982; Loomes and Sugden 1982; Sugden 1985). A proposal to use regret avoidance as a moral principle was put forward by Ernst-Jan Wit (1997). Richard Jeffrey's (1983) criterion of ratifiability should also be mentioned, since it recommends what can be described as hypothetical retrospection with respect to probability assignments.

10. We seem to have a general tendency to avoid situations in which we receive feedback that may give rise to feelings of regret (Zeelenberg et al. 1996; Zeelenberg 1999; Zeelenberg and Pieters 2004). As an example of this, litigants tend to prefer settlement to trial. If you go for settlement, you will never learn what the outcome of a trial would have been, but if you go for trial you will be able to compare its outcome to the settlement that was previously within reach (Guthrie 1999). Active avoidance of feedback information can prevent learning from experience (Russo and Schoemaker 1989, pp. 195–199).
11. Weirich 1981; Williams 1981, pp. 34–36. For a criticism of Williams, see Bittner (1992). For a conceptual clarification of regret and remorse, see Baron (1988).
12. Weber (1998, pp. 105–106) distinguishes between outcome regret that refers to 'how things turned out' and decision-making regret that requires 'that one can, in hindsight, think that one had an available reason at the time of choice to choose other than as one did'. In hypothetical retrospection, only the latter form of regret should be (hypothetically) elicited.
13. Williams 1976.
14. Humberstone 1980; Zeelenberg and Pieters 2007, pp. 4–5.
15. Williams 1976, pp. 130–131; Humberstone 1980; Weirich 1981; Ladmore 1999.
16. This is an instance of the general requirement that rational comparisons should refer to the same aspects of the comparanda. It would be difficult to compare two opera performances if one has only heard a sound recording of one of them and seen a silent film of the other.
17. Cf. the discussion of actualism in Section 2.2.
18. In contrast, it is often reasonable to take predicted or expected future changes in preferences into account. Admittedly, the distinction between moral values and personal preferences is not always crystal-clear.
19. Festinger 1957; Wilson 1971; Mellers and McGraw 2001.
20. Sidgwick [1907] 1962, p. 111.
21. However, it avoids the complications of attempting to achieve 'an objective standpoint detached from the present' (Nagel 1986, p. 132) or any other such abstract construction.

22. Let *A* denote an option in which €10 is received for certain. Let *B* denote an option with a 50 per cent probability of receiving €20 and a 50 per cent probability of receiving nothing. Let *C* denote an option with a 50 per cent probability of receiving €1000 and a 50 per cent probability of having to pay €980. Then *B* is the most risk-taking alternative in a choice between *A* and *B*, but it is the least risk-taking alternative in a choice between *B* and *C*.
23. To see how this affects normative appraisals, let x/A denote that *x* is performed when *A* is the set of alternatives. (We assume that *x* is an element of *A*.) Let us assume that normative appraisals refer to isolated actions, i.e. they are independent of what the other alternatives are. This means that if *x* and *y* are both elements of $A \cap B$, then x/A is normatively superior to y/A if and only if x/B is normatively superior to y/B. As an example of this, if $y/\{x,y\}$ is normatively superior to $x/\{x,y\}$ and $z/\{x,z\}$ is normatively superior to $x/\{x,z\}$, then each of $y/\{x,y,z\}$ and $z/\{x,y,z\}$ is normatively superior to $x/\{x,y,z\}$. This can however be contested in the following example: *x*, *y*, and *z* are three actions on the scene of a severe accident. *x* will save a random victim, whereas *y* will save Yvette, an old acquaintance to whom you feel some gratitude, and *z* will save Zoe, another acquaintance to whom you feel gratitude to the same extent. Arguably, structural considerations should not exclude that (i) $y/\{x,y\}$ is normatively superior to $x/\{x,y\}$ due to your special obligations to Yvette, (ii) $z/\{x,z\}$ is normatively superior to $x/\{x,z\}$ for analogous reasons, but (iii) due to considerations of fairness, $x/\{x,y,z\}$ is not normatively inferior to $y/\{x,y,z\}$ or to $z/\{x,y,z\}$.
24. It is not assumed that the decision has to be morally optimal, or satisfy moral requirements maximally. Hence, scope is left for choice between alternatives that are all acceptable but differ in terms of moral value.
25. Its major competitor, namely expected utility theory as currently applied in risk analysis, is unstable in this sense. Risk analysis seldom resists the strain exerted by the actual occurrence of a serious negative event, even if that event was included in the calculations. This can be seen from the post-accident argumentation after almost any accident. If the expected utility argumentation were followed to the end, then many accidents would be defended as consequences of a maximization of expected utility that is, *in toto*, beneficial. However, this type of reasoning is very rarely heard in practice. Seldom do we hear a company that was responsible for an accident say that the accident was an acceptable part of the maximization of total utility. Instead, they tend to either regret their shortcomings or claim that someone else was responsible for the accident. It should also be noted that accident investigation boards are instructed to answer the questions 'What happened? Why did it happen? How can similar events be avoided in the future?', not the question 'Was the accident defensible in an expected utility calculation?' Once a serious accident has taken place, the application of expected utility maximization appears much less satisfactory than before the accident.
26. Obviously, errors of prediction cannot be avoided. This is a problem shared by all decision rules.
27. As one example of this, the fact that the accident took place may give us a reason to reconsider whether we were justified in believing it to be highly improbable. See Hansson (2009a).
28. Hansson 1999b.

29. To make this more precise (although admittedly somewhat overexact), let there be a set *A* of alternatives and a set *V* of viewpoints. Each viewpoint is constituted by a point in time in a branch of possible future development, as explained above in note 8. Let $f(a,v)$ denote the degree to which the alternative *a* violates moral requirements as seen from the viewpoint *v*. If $f(a,v) = 0$ then *a* does not violate any moral requirement as seen from the viewpoint *v*. We have a moral dilemma if and only if for all $a \in A$ there is some $v \in V$ such that $f(a,v)>0$. The proposed solution is to choose an *a* such that for all $a' \in A: \max_{v \in V}(f(a',v)) \geq \max_{v \in V}(f(a,v))$. For each *a* and *v*, $f(a,v)$ represents an evaluation in which the probabilistic information available at the time of decision can be taken into account.
30. Cf. Section 2.5.
31. In the language of note 29, this corresponds to identifying, for each *a*, the value of $\max_{v \in V}(f(a,v))$which is exactly what we need to apply the decision rule described there.
32. Cf. Section 3.3.
33. Cf. Section 5.2.
34. Godman and Hansson 2009; Jebari and Hansson 2013.
35. An exception must be made if we extend the procedure of hypothetical retrospection to future viewpoints in which the agent is no longer present as a capable reasoner. In such cases, a hypothetical evaluator with the same moral standards as the agent can be used as a heuristic device.

5 Thinking in Uncertain Terms

1. See Sections 1.1 and 2.2.
2. Such a factor may possibly also be present in a real-life version of Example 5.2. There is some evidence that drivers using seat belts drive more carelessly and put pedestrians at greater risk (Janssen 1994), but also some evidence pointing in the other direction (Cohen and Einav, 2003).
3. Hansson 1993.
4. A similar example can be found in Williams (1976, pp. 128–129).
5. Paté-Cornell and Neu 1985.
6. Hansson 1996b.
7. Hansson and Johannesson 1997; Hansson 1999a; Hansson 2006d. – More sophisticated approaches that take into account the uncertainty deriving from the choice between different models and assessments can be found in risk assessments performed in the nuclear sector, but more seldom in other areas such as the risk assessment of chemicals (Rechard 1999).
8. Hansson 2008b. On risk neutrality, see also Hansson and Rudén (2008). For a mathematically precise definition of the concept, see Rothschild and Stiglitz (1970).
9. Hansson 2007a.
10. The scope for such a choice can be created for instance by replacing maximization by satisficing (Slote 1984; Byron 2004), by acknowledging supererogation (Urmson 1958; Hansson 2013c), or by assigning positive value to the individual's free choice of a course of action.

11. In the 1990 report, the 'Business-as-Usual' scenario was estimated to lead to an increase in global mean temperature of about 0.3 °C per decade, with an uncertainty range of 0.2 °C to 0.5 °C (IPCC 1990, p. xxii). In the 2007 report, observed values of about 0.2 °C were reported, and a prognosis of 0.2 °C per decade was given for the next two decades (IPCC 2007, p. 12).
12. Cf. Section 1.2.
13. For a more detailed discussion, see Hansson (2006g).
14. The term 'equipoise' dominates in North America, whereas the term 'uncertainty principle' is commonly used in Europe for approximately the same concept (Weijer et al. 2000).
15. Nothing essential will be changed if we relax that condition. What we need is some reasonable point estimate. The most obvious candidate for the point estimate is the expectation value (probability-weighted value) of the treatment. However, an expectation value can only be calculated if the treatment effect is measured on a cardinal scale. If the scale is not cardinal, then the median of the distribution can serve essentially the same purpose. Other reasonable constructions of point estimates are also possible, such as some percentile lower than the 50th to be employed in cautious decision-making.
16. This can be illustrated with a numerical decision rule, namely the index of (in)cautiousness that was introduced by Daniel Ellsberg ([1961] 1988). For each alternative x, let $exp(x)$ be the expectation value of its outcome (the point estimate) and let $min(x)$ be the lowest value of its outcome that is a serious possibility. Let ρ be a value between 0 and 1 that represents the relative weight that the decision-maker assigns to the expectation value in relation to the lowest seriously possible value. For each alternative, the measure $\rho \times exp(x) + (1-\rho) \times min(x)$ represents its overall value, and the decision rule prescribes that an alternative with as high overall value as possible be chosen. However, decision-makers often do not have a determinate value of ρ. It is more reasonable to assume that there is an interval of such values that are compatible with the decision-makers' indecisiveness. The indeterminateness of ρ then gives rise to the uncertainty needed for clinical equipoise. To make this concrete, assume that the value of ρ vacillates between 0.2 and 0.8. Furthermore, assume that in Figure 5.3, we have (in some arbitrary unit that need not be specified for the present purpose of illustration) $exp(d) = 25$, $min(d) = 22$, $exp(e) = 35$ and $min(e) = 12$. Then there is a reasonable value of ρ (namely $\rho = 0.5$) according to which d and e are of equal value. Thus, given some reasonable degree of cautiousness, there is uncertainty between d and e. Such a situation can be described as one of equipoise. This numerical example is only intended as an illustration of a type of decision criteria that will in practice mostly have to be non-numerical and therefore less exact.

    (Ellsberg called this decision rule an 'optimism-pessimism' index, but that is an unfortunate terminology. A person who is pessimistic with respect to a possible negative event is one who believes that its probability is high or its consequences large, or both. A person who is cautious with respect to that same event is someone who is willing to take significant trouble to decrease its probability or limit its consequences, or both. Pessimism and cautiousness need not coincide.)
17. Cf. Section 1.3.
18. Hansson 2004b.

19. A mere possibility argument may also concern other properties of an action or decision than its consequences. I am not aware that non-consequential mere possibility arguments have been appealed to in practice.
20. Donahoe 1969.
21. Rousseau 1992, pp. 55–67.
22. Hansson 2011a.
23. It was called the 'test of alternative effects' in Hansson (2004b).
24. Hansson 1996a.
25. Ruthen 1993; Ball 2008; Overbye 2008; Ellis et al. 2008.
26. Hansson 2008a.
27. On the notion of stability, see Hansson and Helgesson (2003).

6 Fair Exchanges of Risk

1. Rothschild 1978, p. 717. For critical appraisals of this approach, see Pearce et al. (1981), Bicevskis (1982), and Otway and von Winterfeldt (1982).
2. Fiksel 1985, pp. 257–258. On de minimis risk, see also Rechard (1999, pp. 783–785) and Peterson (2002). On the related sheer size fallacy, see Hansson (2004e).
3. Bicevskis 1982. For discussions of the equally implausible idea that risks smaller than naturally occurring risks are always acceptable, see Hansson (2003b and 2011b).
4. For that conclusion to follow, another premise must be added, namely the premise of interpersonal compensability. Interpersonal comparability does not imply interpersonal compensability. The reason why they have often been conflated may be that they come together both in utilitarianism and in conventional risk analysis (Hansson 2004a).
5. Gilles 1994, pp. 1020 and 1035.
6. Thomson 1986 and 1990; McCarthy 1997; Zimmerman 2008.
7. Hansson 2003a. Related principles have been discussed in the literature: Coburn 1981; Thomson 1990, pp. 228 ff and p. 245; McCarthy 1997; Zimmerman 2006 and 2008, pp. 81–87.
8. In addition, an action that imposes a risk on a person can also be morally wrong for reasons other than that risk imposition.
9. Hansson 1988b; Hansson and Makinson 1997. Cf. Section 2.3.
10. Al-Hibri 1980.
11. Cf. Section 2.3.
12. Goldman 2001, p. 116.
13. The terminology varies in the literature. Girill (1978) uses 'cancel' and 'nullify' for particular subcases of the general case when the defeated obligation has no force left. For a classification of types of defeasance, see Sinnott-Armstrong (1999).
14. Bernard Williams (1973, p. 175) introduced the term 'residual obligation'. See also Pietroski (1993), Brummer (1996), and Hansson and Peterson (2001).
15. Cf. Section 2.3.
16. Cf. Section 2.4 on the implausibility of strictly rights-based moral theories.
17. Hansson 1989a.

18. The earliest systematic treatment of reciprocity in risk impositions that I am aware of is Fletcher's (1972) use of reciprocity in the analysis of tort liability. See also McCarthy (1996).
19. By a social practice is meant, of course, an actually existing social practice. Hence rule (4) does not allow the justification of risk-exposure by reference to a hypothetical social practice that would, if it existed, work to the exposed person's advantage. Real risks cannot be traded for hypothetical benefits.
20. Cf. Lübbe 1998, pp. 186 and 193.
21. This view is inspired by Michael Walzer's (1983) 'complex equality', according to which principles of justice are applied separately and independently in different spheres of society.
22. Scanlon 1998, pp. 206–213; Ashford 2003, pp. 298–300; Lenman 2008, pp. 112–117.
23. However, individual welfare is not a function of the resources available to the individual in question. It is also highly dependent on collective arrangements in society. Therefore, it should not be taken for granted that the members of the higher classes gain in terms of welfare (or health) from an unequal distribution of resources. See Wilkinson and Pickett (2009), Hansson (2004c) and (concerning health) Lochner et al. (2001) and Macinko et al. (2003).
24. Bryant and Mohai 1992; Ringquist 2000; Shrader-Frechette 2002; Messias 2003; Larson et al. 2008; Cranor 2011.
25. On the use of provisional goals see Edvardsson and Hansson (2005, pp. 358–359); Rosencrantz et al. (2007); and Edvardsson (2008).
26. *Exodus* 20:5, King James' Bible.
27. Sin et al. 2003; Buchmueller et al. 2005.
28. See Brighouse and Swift (2008) for a critical discussion of some attempts at such argumentation.
29. Ripstein 1999, p. 54. See also Ronald Dworkin's (1981, pp. 308–312) discussion of the 'starting-gate theory of fairness'.
30. Nozick 1974 and 1989, pp. 286–289.
31. Danley 1978; Lyons 1981; See also Section 2.5.
32. Nagel 1991, p. 71; Segall 2010.
33. Fleurbaey 2001.
34. Another problematic feature of starting line theories becomes apparent as soon as we try to determine the point in time in a person's life when she stands on her starting line. The competition for high grades in college cannot be fair unless the students have the same starting positions. These positions are largely determined by their success in high school, which in turn depends on their results from elementary school, etc. In this way, whatever starting lines are selected, we have compelling reasons to go one step further back and select an earlier point in time. As we go further back towards early childhood, the metaphor of a fair competition gradually loses its credibility. This can be seen from Fishkin's (1983, pp. 57–58) hypothetical 'baby lottery' in which babies are redistributed at random to families immediately after birth. If a baby lottery is introduced into a highly hierarchical society, then there will be large differences in the life chances of babies allotted to different families. It would then be strange to claim that the lottery ensures what we normally mean by equal chances or equal opportunities. Cf. Barry (1988, pp. 31–33).

35. Hansson (2004d).
36. On the connection between consent and veto power, see Fotion (1987) and Hansson (2006b).
37. A reason why clause (i) has to be retained after clause (ii) was added is that the latter clause alone does not offer minority protection.
38. Hansson 1992 and 1996d; Rappeport 2003, pp. 41–42.
39. In a famous speech on 5 February 1794 Robespierre made 'democracy' a central term in the revolutionary vocabulary. In the same speech he also claimed that terror was 'moins un principe particulier, qu'une conséquance du principe général de la démocratie' (less a particular principle than a consequence of the general principle of democracy) (Robespierre [1794] 1967, p. 357; Cf. Christophersen 1966, pp. 7–12).

7 Moral Excuses under Scrutiny

1. Boyle 1997.
2. Weale 1979; Trachtman 1985; Heinzerling 2000.
3. Derek Parfit identified as a 'mistake in moral mathematics' the belief that imperceptible effects are morally negligible (1984, p. 75). His examples are cases of collective action in which the effects of each individual action are imperceptible, whereas their combined effects are clearly noticeable and indeed highly significant from a moral point of view (Cf. Parfit 1986, pp. 846–847; Gruzalski 1986, p. 778; and Klosko 1990, p. 200). It was Kristin Shrader-Frechette (1987, 1988) who showed the relevance of this discussion to health effects of low-dose exposure to radiation and chemicals.
4. Hansson 1999c.
5. This is the classic case of 'statistical victims'.
6. The phrase 'undetectable effects' is used here for convenience in spite of being imprecise. If a cancer develops in a person exposed to radiation from a technical device, but it cannot be detected that the disease is an effect of the exposure, then the cancer itself can all too easily be detected. It is the connection between the exposure and the cancer that is undetectable. It would be more precise to speak of 'undetectable connections' or 'phenomena whose property of being an effect of certain human behaviour is undetectable'. (Parfit 1984, pp. 75–76, misses this distinction when dismissing radiation cases since the effects are perceptible although the causes may be unknown.)
7. Vainio and Tomatis 1985; Hansson 1995, 1997a and 2002a.
8. Hansson 2002b.
9. Rudén and Hansson 2008.
10. Moreno 2001, p. 145.
11. Hansson 1998a, pp. 17–34.
12. Mastromatteo 1981.
13. ACGIH 1991, pp. 1698–1699.
14. Health Physics Society 1996. In 2004, the Society modified this statement, and now said with reference to the same dose levels: 'Below these doses, risk estimates should not be used. Expressions of risk should only be qualitative, that is, a range based on the uncertainties in estimating risk (NCRP

1997) emphasizing the inability to detect any increased health detriment (that is, zero health effects is a likely outcome)' (Health Physics Society 2004). This formulation was retained when the document was again revised in 2010 (Health Physics Society 2010).
15. To simplify the story, the long latency period of actual chemical carcinogenesis is left out.
16. Cottingham 1983, p. 89.
17. Aristotle suggested that a certain measure of philia (friendship) could persist between strangers; he spoke of 'the mutual friendliness between members of the same species, especially of the human species; which is why we commend those who love their fellow men' (Aristotle 1976, p. 258; 1155a20). I am grateful to Barbro Fröding for calling my attention to this passage. See also comments by Irwin in Aristotle (1999, p. 273), and by Whiting (2006, pp. 290–291).
18. Cottingham 1983, p. 97.
19. See for instance Machan's (1987) argumentation against workers' right to occupational safety. For a rebuttal, see Spurgin (2006), and for a historical background, Ellerman (2005).
20. McCarthy 1997, p. 215.
21. Consent as referred to here is not a state of mind but a performative action that can trigger permissions. Cf. Baker 1988 and Brett 1988.
22. Faden and Beauchamp 1986.
23. Exceptions are standardly made for persons who are unable to make autonomous decisions, such as minors, unconscious persons, and persons with a serious mental disease or handicap (Beauchamp and Childress, 2001, pp. 98–104).
24. See Hansson (2006b) for a critical review.
25. According to the Helsinki declaration, the physician who takes part in medical research always has a duty to 'protect the life, health, privacy, and dignity of the human subject'. Informed consent does not absolve her from that duty. http://www.wma.net/e/ethicsunit/helsinki.htm.
26. On the notion of voluntariness, see Olsaretti (1998 and 2008), Peter (2004), Colburn (2008), and Hansson (2007d).
27. Such 'sham surgery' is performed in some clinical trials, but it has been contested on ethical grounds (Albin 2005).
28. Thomson 1986, pp. 189–191. Coleman (1980, 536n-537n) presented a similar example. Real estate prices tend to be low in residential areas with high crime rates. House-buyers are therefore in a sense economically compensated for the higher risk of crime, but it would be strange to claim that they have consented to being burglarized.
29. Hansson, 2006b and 2007c. For an account of decision-making that puts emphasis on the early stages of decision processes, see Condorcet ([1793] 1847, pp. 342–343).
30. Simmons 1987, p. 6.
31. Cf. Perry 2007.
32. Ripstein 1994, p. 21.
33. Taylor 1984. The anti-paternalist argumentation against tobacco restrictions is exemplified by Viscusi (2002).
34. Feinberg 1975; Sartorius 1983; Hansson 2005a.

35. Hansson 2005a.
36. In spite of this, the predominant trend in debates on public policy is to take its validity for granted. This inference has also been surprisingly little discussed by philosophers writing on paternalism. Feinberg is one of the few exceptions. He distinguishes between harms that a person inflicts on herself and harms that others inflict on her with her consent. Feinberg does not make much of the distinction, but he points out that '[a]pplied to voluntary slavery, the principle of non-exploitation might say that it isn't aimed at preventing one man from being slave so much as preventing the other from being a slave-owner' (Feinberg, 1975).
37. Boyle 1997.
38. Leclerc and Herrera 1999; McCrory et al. 2007; Zazryn et al. 2008; Bazarian et al. 2009.
39. Becker 1986; Burris 1997; Needleman 1998.
40. Hansson 2009b.
41. Railton (1986, p. 164), while defending moral realism, conceded that 'one can be serious about morality, even to a fault, without being a moral realist'.

References

Abbott, Philip (1978) 'Philosophers and the abortion question', *Political Theory* 6: 313–35.
ACGIH (1991) *Documentation of the threshold limit values and biological exposure indices*, Sixth edition. Cincinnati: American Conference of Governmental Industrial Hygienists.
Adler, Nancy E. and Judith Stewart (2009) 'Reducing obesity: motivating action while not blaming the victim', *Milbank Quarterly* 87: 49–70.
Albin, R. L. (2005) 'Sham surgery controls are mitigated trolleys', *Journal of Medical Ethics* 31: 149–52.
Al-Hibri, Azizah (1980) 'Conditionality and Ross's deontic distinction', *Southwestern Journal of Philosophy* 11: 79–87.
Altham, J. E. J. (1983) 'Ethics of risk', *Proceedings of the Aristotelian Society* 84: 15–29.
Anand, Paul (1993) *Foundations of rational choice under risk*. Oxford: Clarendon.
Anstey, Peter R. (2002) 'Robert Boyle and the heuristic value of mechanism', *Studies in History and Philosophy of Science* 33: 161–74.
Aquinas, Thomas (1966) *Die Deutsche Thomas-Ausgabe: Vollständige, ungekürzte deutsch-lateinische Ausgabe der Summa theologica*, Bd 17B, *Die Liebe* (2. Teil) ; Klugheit : II-II, 34–56. Josef Endres, ed., Salzburg: Pustet.
Aristotle (1976) *The ethics of Aristotle: The Nicomachean ethics*. Translated by J. A. K. Thomson, revised edition, Harmondsworth: Penguin Books.
Aristotle (1999) *Nicomachean ethics*. Translated with Introduction, Notes, and Glossary, by Terence Irwin. Second Edition. Indianapolis: Hackett Publishing Company.
Ashford, Elizabeth (2003) 'The demandingness of Scanlon's contractualism', *Ethics* 113: 273–302.
Arnauld, Antoine ([1962] 1964) *The art of thinking. Port-Royal logic*, transl. by James Dickoff and Patricia James. Indianapolis: Bobbs-Merrill.
Arnauld, Antoine and Pierre Nicole ([1662] 1965) *La logique ou l'art de penser*, Pierre Clair and François Girbal, eds, Paris: Presses Universitaires de France.
Arrow, Kenneth J (1951) 'Alternative approaches to the theory of choice in risk-taking situations', *Econometrica* 19: 404–37.
Athanassoulis, Nafsika and Allison Ross (2010) 'A virtue ethical account of making decisions about risk', *Journal of Risk Research* 13: 217–30.
Baker, B.M. (1988) 'Consent, assault and sexual assault'. In A. Bayefsky, ed., *Legal theory meets legal practice*. Edmonton: Academic Printing & Publishing. 223–38.
Ball, P. (2008) 'Of myths and men', *Nature News* 2 May 2008. http://www.nature.com/news/2008/080502/full/news.2008.797.html. Accessed in January 2013.
Banja, John (2004) 'Obesity, responsibility and empathy', *Case Manager* 15: 43–6.
Barker, Ernest (1930) 'The authorship of the Vindiciae contra tyrannos', *Cambridge Historical Journal* 3(2): 164–81.

Baron, Marcia (1988) 'Remorse and agent-regret', *Midwest Studies in Philosophy* 13: 259–81.
Barry, B (1988) 'Equal opportunity and moral arbitrariness'. In Norman E. Bowie, ed., *Equal opportunity*. Boulder: Westview Press, 23–44.
Bazarian, J. J., I. Cernak, L. Noble-Haeusslein, S. Potolicchio, and N. Temkin (2009) 'Long-term neurologic outcomes after traumatic brain injury', *Journal of Head Trauma Rehabilitation* 24: 439–51.
Beauchamp, T. L. and Childress J. F. (2001) *Principles of biomedical ethics*, 5th ed. New York: Oxford University Press.
Becker, M. H. (1986) 'The tyranny of health promotion', *Public Health Reviews* 14: 15–25.
Bell, D.E. (1982) 'Regret in decision making under uncertainty', *Operations Research* 30: 961–81.
Bengtsson, Lennart (2006) 'Geo-engineering to confine climate change: is it at all feasible?', *Climatic Change* 77: 229–34.
Bennett, Jonathan (1995) *The act itself*. Oxford: Clarendon Press.
Berger, Ruth (1998) 'Understanding science: why causes are not enough', *Philosophy of Science* 65: 306–32.
Bernoulli, Daniel (1738) 'Specimen theoriae novae de mensura sortis'. *Commentarii Academiae Scientarium Imperialis Petropolitanae* 5: 175–92.
Bernoulli, Daniel ([1738] 1954) 'Exposition of a new theory on the measurement of risk', *Econometrica* 22: 23–36.
Bicevskis, A. (1982) 'Unacceptability of acceptable risk', *Search* 13(1–2): 31–4.
Bittner, Rüdiger (1992) 'Is it reasonable to regret things one did?', *Journal of Philosophy* 89: 262–73.
Biwer, B. M. and J. P. Butler (1999) 'Vehicle emission unit risk factors for transportation risk assessments', *Risk Analysis* 19: 1157–71.
Bondi, H. (1985) 'Risk in perspective', In M.G. Cooper, ed. *Risk. Man-made hazard to man*. Oxford: Clarendon, 8–17.
Bordley, Robert F. and Gordon Hazen (1992) 'Nonlinear utility models arising from unmodelled small world intercorrelations', *Management Science* 38: 1010–17.
Boyle, P. (1997) 'Cancer, cigarette smoking and premature death in Europe: a review including the Recommendations of European Cancer Experts Consensus Meeting, Helsinki, October 1996.' *Lung Cancer* 17(1): 1–60.
Bradley, Ben (2005) 'Virtue consequentialism', *Utilitas* 17: 282–98.
Brandt, Richard B (1965) 'The concepts of obligation and duty', *Mind* 73: 374–93.
Brett, N. (1988) 'Commentary'. In A. Bayefsky, ed. *Legal theory meets legal practice*. Edmonton: Academic Printing & Publishing. 253–57.
Brighouse, Harry and Adam Swift (2008) 'Putting educational equality in its place', *Education Finance and Policy* 3: 444–66.
Brink, David O. (1986) 'Utilitarian morality and the personal point of view', *Journal of Philosophy* 83: 417–38.
Broad, C.D. ([1914] 1971) 'The doctrine of consequences in ethics', reprinted in D.R. Cheney (ed.) *Broad's critical essays in moral philosophy*. London: George Allen and Unwin, 17–42.
Broome, John (1978) 'Trying to value a life', *Journal of Public Economics* 9: 91–100.

Feinberg, J. (1975) 'Legal paternalism'. In Wasserstrom, R. (ed.) *Today's moral problems*. New York: MacMillan Publishing. 33–50.
Feldman, Fred (2006) 'Actual utility, the objection from impracticality, and the move to expected utility', *Philosophical Studies* 129: 49–79.
Festinger, Leon (1957). *A theory of cognitive dissonance*. Stanford, CA: Stanford University Press.
Fiksel, J. (1985) 'Toward a de minimis policy in risk regulation', *Risk Analysis* 5: 257–9.
Finkelstein, Claire (2003) 'Is risk a harm?', *University of Pennsylvania Law Review* 151: 963–1001.
Fischhoff, Baruch, Sarah Lichtenstein, Paul Slovic, Stephen L. Derby, and Ralph L. Keeney (1981) *Acceptable risk*. Cambridge: Cambridge University Press.
Fishkin, J. S. (1983) *Justice, equal opportunity, and the family*. New Haven: Yale University Press.
Fletcher, George (1972) 'Fairness and utility in tort theory', *Harvard Law Review* 85: 537–73.
Fleurbaey, Marc (2001) 'Egalitarian opportunities', *Law and Philosophy* 20: 499–530.
Fotion, Nicholas (1987) 'Simmons and the concept of consent: commentary on "Consent and fairness in planning land use"', *Business and Professional Ethics Journal* 6(2): 21–4.
Frankena, W.K. (1952) 'The concept of universal human rights'. In *Science, language and human rights*, American Philosophical Association, Eastern Division, vol 1, Philadelphia. 189–207.
Fried, Barbara H. (2012) 'Can contractualism save us from aggregation?', *Journal of Ethics* 16: 39–66.
Fried, Charles (1978) *Right and wrong*. Cambridge, Mass.: Harvard University Press.
Garvin, Lucius (1953) *A modern introduction to ethics*. Cambridge, Mass.: Riverside Press.
Gauthier, David (1986) *Morals by agreement*. Oxford: Clarendon Press.
Gibbard, Allan and William Harper (1988) 'Counterfactuals and two kinds of expected utility'. In Peter Gärdenfors and Nils-Eric Sahlin, eds, *Decision, probability and utility: Selected readings*. New York, NY: Cambridge University Press. 341–76.
Gilles, S.G. (1994) 'The invisible hand formula', *Virginia Law Review* 80: 1015–54.
Girill, T. R. (1978) 'On the defeasibility of duties', *Journal of Value Inquiry* 12: 197–209.
Godman, Marion and Sven Ove Hansson (2009) 'European public advice on nanobiotechnology – four convergence seminars', *Nanoethics* 3: 43–59.
Goldman, Alan H. (2001) 'Moral reasoning without rules', *Mind & Society* 2(4): 105–18.
Graham, John D and Jonathan Baert Wiener (1995) *Risk versus risk: Tradeoffs in protecting health and the environment*. Cambridge Mass.: Harvard University Press.
Griffin, Dale and Lyle Brenner (2004) 'Perspectives on probability judgment calibration'. In Derek. J. Koehler and Nigel Harvey (eds), *Blackwell handbook of judgment and decision making*. Malden, MA: Blackwell. 177–191.

Gruzalski, Bart (1986) 'Parfit's impact on utilitarianism', *Ethics* 96: 760–83.
Guay, Robert (2005) 'A refutation of consequentialism', *Metaphilosophy* 36: 348–62.
Gustafsson, Johan (2010) 'Freedom of choice and expected compromise', *Social Choice and Welfare* 35: 65–79.
Guthrie, Chris (1999) 'Better settle than sorry: the regret aversion theory of litigation behavior', *University of Illinois Law Review* 43–90.
Hall, Ned (2000) 'Causality and the price of transitivity', *Journal of Philosophy* 97: 198–222.
Hamlin, Alan P. (1989) 'Rights, indirect utilitarianism, and contractarianism', *Economics and Philosophy* 5: 167–87.
Hansson, Sven Ove (1988a) 'Deontic logic without misleading alethic analogies – Part I', *Logique et Analyse* 31: 337–53.
Hansson, Sven Ove (1988b) 'Deontic logic without misleading alethic analogies – Part II', *Logique et Analyse* 31: 355–70.
Hansson, Sven Ove (1989a) 'Dimensions of risk', *Risk Analysis* 9: 107–12.
Hansson, Sven Ove (1989b) 'Preference logic as a model for risk comparisons'. In *Proceedings, management of risk from genotoxic substances in the environment: symposium*, Stockholm. 355–364.
Hansson, Sven Ove (1991) 'Norms and values', *Critica* 23(67): 3–13.
Hansson, Sven Ove (1992) 'A procedural model of voting', *Theory and Decision* 32: 269–301.
Hansson, Sven Ove (1993) 'The false promises of risk analysis', *Ratio* 6: 16–26.
Hansson, Sven Ove (1995) 'The detection level', *Regulatory Toxicology and Pharmacology* 22: 103–9.
Hansson, Sven Ove (1996a) 'Decision-making under great uncertainty', *Philosophy of the Social Sciences* 26: 369–86.
Hansson, Sven Ove (1996b) 'What is philosophy of risk?', *Theoria* 62: 169–86.
Hansson, Sven Ove (1996c) 'Legal relations and potestative rules', *Archiv für Rechts- und Sozialphilosophie* 82: 266–74.
Hansson, Sven Ove (1996d) 'Social choice with procedural preferences', *Social Choice and Welfare* 13: 215–30.
Hansson, Sven Ove (1997a) 'Can we reverse the burden of proof?', *Toxicology Letters* 90: 223–28.
Hansson, Sven Ove (1997b) 'The limits of precaution', *Foundations of Science* 2: 293–306.
Hansson, Sven Ove (1998a) *Setting the limit: Occupational health standards and the limits of science*. New York: Oxford University Press.
Hansson, Sven Ove (1998b) 'Should we avoid moral dilemmas?', *Journal of Value Inquiry* 32: 407–16.
Hansson, Sven Ove (1999a) 'Adjusting scientific practices to the precautionary principle', *Human and Ecological Risk Assessment* 5: 909–21.
Hansson, Sven Ove (1999b) 'But what should I do?', *Philosophia* 27: 433–40.
Hansson, Sven Ove (1999c) 'The moral significance of indetectable effects', *Risk* 10: 101–8.
Hansson, Sven Ove (1999d) 'A philosophical perspective on risk', *Ambio*, 28: 539–42.
Hansson, Sven Ove (1999e) *A textbook of belief dynamics: Theory change and database updating*. Dordrecht: Kluwer.

Hansson, Sven Ove (2001a) *The structure of values and norms*. Cambridge: Cambridge University Press.
Hansson, Sven Ove (2001b) 'The modes of value', *Philosophical Studies* 104: 33–46.
Hansson, Sven Ove (2002a) 'Replacing the No Effect Level (NOEL) with Bounded Effect Levels (OBEL and LEBEL)', *Statistics in Medicine*, 21: 3071–3078.
Hansson, Sven Ove (2002b) 'Uncertainties in the knowledge society', *Social Science Journal* 171: 39–46.
Hansson, Sven Ove (2003a) 'Ethical criteria of risk acceptance', *Erkenntnis* 59: 291–309.
Hansson, Sven Ove (2003b) 'Are natural risks less dangerous than technological risks?', *Philosophia Naturalis* 40: 43–54.
Hansson, Sven Ove (2003c) 'Ten philosophical problems in belief revision', *Journal of Logic and Computation* 13: 37–49.
Hansson, Sven Ove (2004a) 'Weighing risks and benefits', *Topoi* 23: 145–52.
Hansson, Sven Ove (2004b) 'Great uncertainty about small things', *Techne* 8(2): 26–35. Also published in Joachim Schummer and Davis Baird, eds, *Nanotechnology challenges: Implications for philosophy, ethics and society*, Singapore: World Scientific Publishing, 2006, 315–325.
Hansson, Sven Ove (2004c) 'Welfare, justice, and Pareto efficiency', *Ethical Theory and Moral Practice* 7: 361–80.
Hansson, Sven Ove (2004d) 'What are opportunities and why should they be equal?', *Social Choice and Welfare* 22: 305–16.
Hansson, Sven Ove (2004e) 'Fallacies of risk', *Journal of Risk Research*, 7: 353–60.
Hansson, Sven Ove (2005a) 'Extended antipaternalism', *Journal of Medical Ethics* 31: 97–100.
Hansson, Sven Ove (2005b) 'Seven myths of risk', *Risk Management*, 7(2): 7–17.
Hansson, Sven Ove (2006a) 'Ideal worlds – wishful thinking in deontic logic', *Studia Logica* 82: 329–36.
Hansson, Sven Ove (2006b) 'Informed consent out of context', *Journal of Business Ethics* 63: 149–54.
Hansson, Sven Ove (2006c) 'Condensed examples in philosophy', *Theoria* 72: 97–9.
Hansson, Sven Ove (2006d) 'Economic (ir)rationality in risk analysis', *Economics and Philosophy* 22: 231–41.
Hansson, Sven Ove (2006e) 'How to define – a tutorial', *Princípios, Revista de Filosofia* 13(19–20): 5–30.
Hansson, Sven Ove (2006f) 'The modal status of philosophy', *Theoria* 72: 173–6.
Hansson, Sven Ove (2006g) 'Uncertainty and the ethics of clinical trials', *Theoretical Medicine and Bioethics* 27: 149–67.
Hansson, Sven Ove (2006h) 'Levi's ideals'. In Erik J. Olsson, ed., *Knowledge and inquiry: Essays on the pragmatism of Isaac Levi*. Cambridge: Cambridge University Press. 241–7.
Hansson, Sven Ove (2007a) 'Hypothetical retrospection', *Ethical Theory and Moral Practice* 10: 145–57.
Hansson, Sven Ove (2007b) 'Philosophical problems in cost-benefit analysis', *Economics and Philosophy* 23: 163–83.
Hansson, Sven Ove (2007c) 'Social decisions about risk and risk-taking', *Social Choice and Welfare* 29: 649–63.

Hansson, Sven Ove (2007d) 'Risk and ethics: three approaches'. In Tim Lewens, ed., *Risk: Philosophical perspectives*. London: Routledge. 21–35.

Hansson, Sven Ove (2007e) 'Risk', *Stanford Encyclopedia of Philosophy*, http://plato.stanford.edu/entries/risk/.

Hansson, Sven Ove (2007f) 'Ethics and radiation protection', *Journal of Radiological Protection* 27: 147–56.

Hansson, Sven Ove (2008a) 'Regulating BFRs – from science to policy', *Chemosphere* 73: 144–7.

Hansson, Sven Ove (2008b) 'Do we need second-order probabilities?', *Dialectica* 62: 525–33.

Hansson, Sven Ove (2009a) 'Measuring uncertainty', *Studia Logica* 93: 21–40.

Hansson, Sven Ove (2009b) 'Ethics beyond application'. In T. Takala, P. Herissone-Kelly and S. Holm (eds) *Cutting through the surface: Philosophical approaches to bioethics*, Amsterdam and New York: Rodopi. 19–28.

Hansson, Sven Ove (2009c) 'From the casino to the jungle: Dealing with uncertainty in technological risk management', *Synthese* 168: 423–32.

Hansson, Sven Ove (2009d) 'Risk and safety in technology'. In Anthonie Meijers (ed.), *Handbook of the philosophy of science*, Volume 9: *Philosophy of technology and engineering sciences*. Elsevier. 1069–102

Hansson, Sven Ove (2009e) 'Should we protect the most sensitive people?', *Journal of Radiological Protection* 29: 211–18.

Hansson, Sven Ove (2010a) 'Risk – objective or subjective, facts or values?', *Journal of Risk Research*, 13: 231–8.

Hansson, Sven Ove (2010b) 'The harmful influence of decision theory on ethics', *Ethical Theory and Moral Practice* 13: 585–93.

Hansson, Sven Ove (2010c) 'Promoting inherent safety', *Process Safety and Environmental Protection* 88: 168–72.

Hansson, Sven Ove (2010d) 'L'incertitude en matière de technologie', *Annales des Mines* 57: 70–4.

Hansson, Sven Ove (2011a) 'Coping with the unpredictable effects of future technologies', *Philosophy and Technology* 24: 137–49.

Hansson, Sven Ove (2011b) 'Radiation protection – sorting out the arguments', *Philosophy and Technology* 24: 363–8.

Hansson, Sven Ove (2012a) 'Safety is an inherently inconsistent concept', *Safety Science* 50: 1522–7.

Hansson, Sven Ove (2012b) 'A panorama of the philosophy of risk'. In Sabine Roeser et al. (eds), *Handbook of risk theory*. Dordrecht: Springer. 27–54.

Hansson, Sven Ove (2012c) 'The trilemma of moral preparedness', *Review Journal of Political Philosophy* 9: 1–5.

Hansson, Sven Ove (2013a) 'The moral oracle's test', *Ethical Theory and Moral Practice*, in press.

Hansson, Sven Ove (2013b) 'Alternative semantics for deontic logic', to be published in Dov Gabbay, John Horty, Ron van der Meyden, and Leon van der Torre (eds), *Handbook on Deontic Logic and Normative Systems*. London: College Publications.

Hansson, Sven Ove (2013c) 'Representing supererogation', *Journal of Logic and Computation*, in press.

Hansson, Sven Ove and Gert Helgesson (2003) 'What is stability', *Synthese* 136(2): 219–35.

Hansson, Sven Ove and Mikael Johannesson (1997) 'Decision-theoretic approaches to global climate change'. In Gunnar Fermann, ed., *International politics of climate change*. Oslo: Scandinavian University Press. 153–78.

Hansson, Sven Ove and David Makinson (1997) 'Applying normative rules with restraint'. In M.L. Dalla Chiara et al., eds, *Logic and scientific method*. Dordrecht: Kluwer. 313–332.

Hansson, Sven Ove and Martin Peterson (2001) 'Rights, risks, and residual obligations', *Risk Decision and Policy* 6: 1–10.

Hansson, Sven Ove and Christina Rudén (2008) 'A risk-neutral default for chemical risk management', *American Journal of Industrial Medicine* 51: 964–7.

Hardin, Russell (1989) 'Ethics and stochastic processes', *Social Philosophy and Policy* 7: 69–80.

Hare, R. M. (1973a) 'Rawls's theory of justice – I', *Philosophical Quarterly* 23: 144–55.

Hare, R. M. (1973b) 'Rawls's theory of justice – II', *Philosophical Quarterly* 23: 241–52.

Harrison, J. (1953) 'Utilitarianism, universalisation, and our duty to be just', *Proceedings of the Aristotelian Society* 53: 105–34.

Harsanyi, J.C. (1953) 'Cardinal utility in welfare economics and in the theory of risk-taking', *Journal of Political Economy* 61: 434–5.

Harsanyi, J.C. (1955) 'Cardinal welfare, individualistic ethic, and interpersonal comparison of utility', *Journal of Political Economy* 63: 309–21.

Harsanyi, J.C. (1975) 'Can the maximin principle serve as a basis for morality – Critique of Rawls, J. theory', *American Political Science Review* 69(2): 594–606.

Hausman, Daniel M. and James Woodward (1999) 'Independence, invariance and the causal Markov condition', *British Journal for the Philosophy of Science* 50: 521–83.

Hayenhjelm, Madeleine and Jonathan Wolff (2012) 'The moral problem of risk impositions: A survey of the literature', *European Journal of Philosophy* 20: e26–e51.

Healey, Richard (1994) 'Non-separable processes and causal explanation', *Studies in History and Philosophy of Science* 25: 337–74.

Health Physics Society (1996) *Radiation risk in perspective*. Position statement of the Health Physics Society, adopted January 1996. Downloaded in December 1998 from http://www2.org/hps/rad.htm.

Health Physics Society (2004) *Radiation risk in perspective*. Position statement of the Health Physics Society, revised August 2004. Downloaded in March 2007 from http://www.hps.org.

Health Physics Society (2010) *Radiation risk in perspective*. Position statement of the Health Physics Society, revised July 2010. Downloaded in May 2012 from http://www.hps.org.

Heinzerling, Lisa (2000) 'The rights of statistical people', *Harvard Environmental Law Review* 24: 189–207.

Hermansson, Hélène and Sven Ove Hansson (2007) 'A three party model tool for ethical risk analysis', *Risk Management* 9: 129–44.

Hesslow, Germund (1981) 'The transitivity of causation', *Analysis* 41: 130–3.

Hobbes, Thomas ([1651] 2012) *Leviathan* I-III.Ed.Noel Malcolm. *Clarendon Edition of the works of Thomas Hobbes*. Oxford: Clarendon Press.

Hoover, Kevin D (1990) 'The logic of causal inference', *Economics and Philosophy* 6: 207–34.
Höpfl, Harro and Martyn P. Thompson (1979) 'The history of contract as a motif in political thought', *American Historical Review* 84: 919–44.
Howe, Roger E. and John E. Roemer (1981) 'Rawlsian justice as the core of a game', *American Economic Review* 71: 880–95.
Humberstone, I. L. (1980) 'You'll regret it', *Analysis* 40: 175–6.
Hynes, M. and E. Vanmarcke (1976) 'Reliability of embankment performance predictions', *Proceedings of the ASCE Engineering Mechanics Division, Specialty Conference*, Waterloo, Ontario, Canada, University of Waterloo Press.
International Organization for Standardization (2002) *Risk management – Vocabulary – Guidelines for use in standards*, ISO/IEC Guide 73.
IPCC (1990) *Climate change: The IPCC scientific assessment*. J.T. Houghton, G.J. Jenkins, and J.J. Ephraums, eds, Cambridge: Cambridge University Press.
IPCC (2007) *Climate change 2007: The physical science basis:. Contribution of Working Group I to the fourth assessment report of the IPCC*. New York: Cambridge University Press.
Jackson, Frank and Robert Pargetter (1986) 'Oughts, options and actualism', *Philosophical Review* 95: 233–55.
Janssen, Wiel (1994) 'Seat-belt wearing and driving behavior: an instrumented-vehicle study', *Accident Analysis and Prevention* 26: 249–61.
Jebari, Karim and Sven Ove Hansson (2013) 'European public deliberation on brain machine interface technology – five convergence seminars', *Science and Engineering Ethics*, in press.
Jeffrey, Richard C. (1956) 'Valuation and acceptance of scientific hypotheses', *Philosophy of Science* 23: 237–49.
Jeffrey, Richard C. (1983) *The logic of decision*, 2nd ed. Chicago: University of Chicago Press.
Kagan, S. (1989) *The limits of morality*. Oxford: Clarendon Press.
Kamm, Frances Myrna (1985) 'Supererogation and obligation', *Journal of Philosophy* 82: 118–38.
Kant, Immanuel ([1797] 1912) 'Über ein vermeintes Recht aus Menschenliebe zu lügen'. In Immanuel Kant, *Gesammelte Schriften* (Akademie-Ausgabe), Abt. 1, Bd 8. Berlin: Königliche Preußische Akademie der Wissenschaften. 423–430.
Kant, Immanuel (1996) *Practical philosophy*. Translated and edited by Mary J. Gregor. The Cambridge edition of the works of Immanuel Kant. Cambridge: Cambridge University Press.
Kernohan, Andrew (2000) 'Individual acts and accumulative consequences', *Philosophical Studies* 97: 343–66.
Keynes, J. M. (1921) *A treatise on probability*. London: Macmillan.
Klemm, Peter G. (1989) 'Risiko – Gedanken zu einer Begriffspräzisierung', *Deutsche Zeitschrift für Philosophie* 37: 348–50.
Klibanoff, Peter (2001) 'Characterizing uncertainty aversion through preference for mixtures', *Social Choice and Welfare* 18: 289–301.
Klosko, George (1990) 'Parfit's moral arithmetic and the obligation to obey the law', *Canadian Journal of Philosophy* 20: 191–214.
Knight, F. H. ([1921] 1935) *Risk, uncertainty and profit*. Boston: Houghton Mifflin.
Knuutila, Simo (1981) 'Deontic logic in the fourteenth century'. In Risto Hilpinen (ed.) *New studies in deontic logic*. Dordrecht: Reidel. 37–85.

Kolm, Serge-Christophe (1998) 'Chance and justice: Social policies and the Harsanyi-Vickrey-Rawls problem', *European Economic Review* 42: 1393–416.

Kress, Ken (1995) 'The seriousness of harm thesis for abnormally dangerous activities'. In David G. Owen, *Philosophical foundations of tort law*. Oxford: Clarendon Press. 277–297.

Kuhn, Thomas S. (1971) 'La notion de causalité dans le devéloppement de la physique'. In M. Bunge (ed.) *Les théories de la causalité*. Paris: Presses univ. de France. 4–15.

Kumar, Rahul (2003) 'Who can be wronged?', *Philosophy and Public Affairs* 31: 99–118.

Kupperman, Joel J (1980) 'Vulgar consequentialism', *Mind* 89: 321–37.

Kvart, Igal (1991) 'Transitivity and preemption of causal relevance', *Philosophical Studies* 64: 125–60.

Lackey, D. (1976) 'Empirical disconfirmation and ethical counter-example', *Journal of Value Inquiry* 10: 30–4.

Ladmore, Charles (1999) 'The idea of a life plan', *Social Philosophy and Policy* 16: 96–112.

Larson, K., S. A. Russ, J. J. Crall, and N. Halfon (2008) 'Influence of multiple social risks on children's health', *Pediatrics* 121: 337–44.

Leclerc, S. and C. D. Herrera (1999) 'Sports medicine and the ethics of boxing', *British Journal of Sports Medicine* 33: 426–9.

Lee, Jig-chuen (1988) 'The nontransitivity of causation', *American Philosophical Quarterly* 25: 87–94.

Leibniz, Gottfried Wilhelm ([1704] 1962) *Sämtliche Schriften und Briefe*, Herausgegeben von der Deutschen Akademie der Wissenschaften zu Berlin, Sechste Reihe, Philosophische Schriften, vol. 6. Berlin: Akademie-Verlag.

Leibniz, Gottfried Wilhelm ([1704] 1996) *New essays on human understanding*, translated and edited by Peter Remnant and Jonathan Bennett. Cambridge: Cambridge University Press.

Lenman, James (2000) 'Consequentialism and cluelessness', *Philosophy and Public Affairs* 29: 342–70.

Lenman, James (2008) 'Contractualism and risk imposition', *Politics, Philosophy and Economics* 7: 99–122.

Leonard, Herman B. and Richard J. Zeckhauser (1986) 'Cost-benefit analysis applied to risk: Its philosophy and legitimacy'. In Douglas MacLean, *Values at risk*. Savage, Maryland: Rowman & Littlefield. 31–48.

Levi, Don S. (1987) 'Hypothetical cases and abortions', *Social Theory and Practice* 13: 17–48.

Lichtenstein, Sarah et al. (1982) 'Calibration of probabilities: The state of the art to 1980'. In Daniel Kahneman, Paul Slovic, and Amos Tversky, eds, *Judgment under uncertainty, heuristics and biases*. Cambridge: Cambridge University Press. 306–34.

Lochner, Kim, Elsie Pamuk, Diane Makuc, Bruce P. Kennedy, and Ichiro Kawachi (2001) 'State-level income inequality and individual mortality risk: a prospective, multi-level study', *American Journal of Public Health* 91: 385–91.

Lockhart, T. (2000) *Moral uncertainty and its consequences*. New York: Oxford University Press.

Lomasky, Loren E. (1978) 'Is actual consequence utilitarianism incoherent?', *Southern Journal of Philosophy* 16: 71–8.

Loomes, G. and R. Sugden (1982) 'Regret theory: an alternative theory of rational choice under uncertainty', *Economic Journal* 92: 805–24.
Louise, Jennie (2004) 'Relativity of value and the consequentialist umbrella', *Philosophical Quarterly* 54: 518–36.
Lübbe, Weyma (1998) *Verantwortung in komplexen kulturellen Prozesssen*. München: Verlag Karl Alber Freiburg.
Luce, R. Duncan and Howard Raiffa (1957) *Games and decisions: Introduction and critical survey*. New York: Wiley.
Lucey, K. G. (1976) 'Counter-examples and borderline cases', *Personalist* 57: 351–5.
Lyons, David (1981) 'The new Indian claims and original rights to land', pp. 355–379 in Jeffrey Paul, ed., *Reading Nozick: Essays on* Anarchy, state, and Utopia. Totowa, N.J.: Rowman & Littlefield.
Machan, T. R. (1987) 'Human rights, workers' rights, and the "right" to occupational safety'. In G. Ezorsky, ed., *Moral rights in the workplace*. Albany: State University of New York Press. 45–50.
Macinko, James A., Leiyu Shi, Barbara Starfield, and John T. Wulu (2003) 'Income inequality and health: a critical review of the literature', *Medical Care Research and Review* 60: 407–52.
Mackie, John L. (1974) *The cement of the universe: a study of causation*. Oxford: Clarendon.
Marcus, Ruth Barcan (1980) 'Moral dilemmas and consistency', *Journal of Philosophy* 77: 121–36.
Mastromatteo, Ernest (1981) 'On the concept of threshold', *American Industrial Hygiene Association Journal* 42: 763–70.
McCarthy, David (1996) 'Liability and risk', *Philosophy and Public Affairs* 25: 238–62.
McCarthy, David (1997) 'Rights, explanation, and risk', *Ethics* 107: 205–25.
McCrory, Paul, Tsharni Zazryn and Peter A. Cameron (2007) 'The evidence for chronic traumatic encephalopathy in boxing', *Sports Medicine* 37: 467–76.
McKerlie, Dennis (1986) 'Rights and risk', *Canadian Journal of Philosophy* 16: 239–51.
Mellers, B. A. and A. P. McGraw (2001) 'Anticipated emotions as guides to choice', *Current Directions in Psychological Science* 10: 210–14.
Messias, Erick (2003) 'Income inequality, illiteracy rate, and life expectancy in Brazil', *American Journal of Public Health* 93: 1294–6.
Mill, John Stuart ([1843] 1996) *A system of logic*. In: *Collected works of John Stuart Mill*. vol 7. London: Routledge.
Mo Tzu (1963) *Basic writings*, Translated by Burton Watson. New York: Columbia University Press.
Moore, G. E. ([1912] 1958) *Ethics*. London: Oxford University Press.
Moreno, Jonathan D. (2001) *Undue risk: Secret state experiments on humans*. New York: Routledge.
Morton, Adam (1991) *Disasters and dilemmas: Strategies for real-life decision making*. Oxford: Basil Blackwell.
Mosley, Albert (2004) 'Does HIV or poverty cause AIDS? Biomedical and epidemiological perspectives', *Theoretical Medicine* 25: 399–421.
Mulvaney, Robert J. (1992) 'Wisdom, time, and avarice in St Thomas Aquinas's treatise on prudence', *Modern Schoolman* 69: 443–62.

Nagel, Thomas (1970) *The possibility of altruism*. Oxford: Clarendon Press.
Nagel, Thomas (1986) *The view from nowhere*. New York: Oxford University Press.
Nagel, Thomas (1991) *Equality and partiality*. New York: Oxford University Press.
National Research Council (NRC) (1983) *Risk assessment in the federal government: Managing the process*. Washington, D.C.: National Academies Press.
Needleman H. L. (1998) 'Childhood lead poisoning: the promise and abandonment of primary prevention', *American Journal of Public Health* 88: 1871–7.
Nickel, James W. (1982) 'Are human rights utopian?', *Philosophy and Public Affairs* 11: 246–64.
Nida-Rümelin, Julian, Johann Schulenburg and Benjamin Rath (2012) *Risikoethik*. Berlin: De Gruyter.
Nozick, Robert (1974) *Anarchy, state, and utopia*. New York: Basic Books.
Nozick, Robert (1989) *The examined life: Philosophical meditations*. New York: Simon & Schuster.
Oberdiek, John (2009) 'Towards a right against risking', *Law and Philosophy* 28: 367–92.
Oberdiek, John (2012) 'The moral significance of risking', *Legal Theory* 18: 339–56.
O'Brien, Jonathan and Timothy Folta (2009) 'Sunk costs, uncertainty and market exit: A real options perspective', *Industrial and Corporate Change* 18: 807–33.
Okasha, Samir (2007) 'Rational choice, risk aversion, and evolution', *Journal of Philosophy* 104: 217–35.
Okasha, Samir (2011) 'Optimal choice in the face of risk: decision theory meets evolution', *Philosophy of Science* 78: 83–104.
Olsaretti, Serena (1998) 'Freedom, force and choice: against the rights-based definition of voluntariness', *Journal of Political Philosophy* 6: 53–78.
Olsaretti, Serena (2008) 'Debate: the concept of voluntariness–a reply', *Journal of Political Philosophy* 16: 112–21.
Oppenheimer, Robert (1980) *Letters and recollections*, ed. Alice Kimball Smith and Charles Weiner. London: Harvard University Press.
O'Riordan, T. and J. Cameron (eds), (1994) *Interpreting the precautionary principle*. London: Earthscan.
O'Riordan, T., J. Cameron, and A. Jordan (eds) (2001) *Reinterpreting the precautionary principle*. London: Cameron May.
Österberg, Jan (1989) 'One more turn on the lawn'. In Sten Lindström and Wlodek Rabinowicz, (eds), *In so many words: Philosophical essays dedicated to Sven Danielsson on the occasion of his fiftieth birthday*. Uppsala: Uppsala University, Department of Philosophy. 125–33.
Otway, Harry J. and Detlof von Winterfeldt (1982) 'Beyond acceptable risk: on the social acceptability of technologies', *Policy Sciences* 14: 247–56.
Overbye, D. (2008) 'Gauging a collider's odds of creating a black hole', *New York Times*, 15 April 2008. http://www.nytimes.com/2008/04/15/science/15risk.html. Accessed in January 2013.
Parfit, Derek (1984) *Reasons and persons*. Oxford: Clarendon Press.
Parfit, Derek (1986) 'Comments', *Ethics* 96: 832–72.
Parfit, Derek (1997) 'Equality and priority', *Ratio* 10: 202–21.
Paté-Cornell, M. E. and J. E. Neu (1985) 'Warning systems and defense policy: a reliability model for the command and control of U.S. nuclear forces', *Risk Analysis* 5: 121–38.

Pattanaik, P. K. and Y. Xu (1990) 'On ranking opportunity sets in terms of freedom of choice', *Recherches Économiques de Louvain* 56: 383–90.

Pattanaik, P. K. and Y. Xu (2000) 'On ranking opportunity sets in economic environment', *Journal of Economic Theory* 93: 48–71.

Pearce, D. W., S. Russell, and R. F. Griffiths (1981) 'Risk assessment: use and misuse' *Proceedings of the Royal Society of London. Series A, Mathematical and Physical Sciences* 376(1764): 181–92.

Perry, Stephen (2007) 'Risk, harm, interests, and rights,'. In Tim Lewens, ed. *Risk: Philosophical perspectives*. London: Routledge. 190–209.

Peter, Fabienne (2004) 'Choice, consent, and the legitimacy of market transactions', *Economics and Philosophy* 20: 1–18.

Peterson, Martin (2002) 'What is a de minimis risk?', *Risk Management* 4: 47–55.

Pettit, Philip (1988) 'The consequentialist can recognize rights', *Philosophical Quarterly* 38: 42–55.

Pietroski, P. (1993) 'Prima facie obligations: ceteris paribus laws in moral theory', *Ethics* 103: 489–515.

Plato (1997) *Protagoras*. In Plato, *Complete Works*, ed. John M. Cooper. Indianapolis, Ind.: Hachett.

Pontzen, Henrik (2007) *Risikoethik: Vom klugen Umgang mit moralisch relevanten Risiken*. Bonn: Universität Bonn.

Portmore, Douglas W. (2007) 'Consequentializing moral theories', *Pacific Philosophical Quarterly* 88: 39–73.

Price, Terry L. (1999) 'Egalitarian justice, luck, and the costs of chosen ends', *American Philosophical Quarterly* 36: 267–78.

Prior, A. N. (1956) 'The consequences of actions', *Proceedings of the Aristotelian Society, Supplement* 30: 91–99.

Pyle, Andrew (2002) 'Boyle on science and the mechanical philosophy: a reply to Chalmers', *Studies in History and Philosophy of Science'* 33: 175–90.

Quine, W. V. (1972) Review of Milton K. Munitz, *Identity and individuation, Journal of Philosophy* 69: 488–97.

Rabinowicz, Wlodek (2002). 'Does practical deliberation crowd out self-prediction?' *Erkenntnis* 57: 91–122.

Railton, Peter (1983) 'Locke, stock, and peril'. In Mary Gibson, ed., *To breathe freely: Risk, consent, and air*. Totowa, N.J.: Rowman & Allanheld. 89–123.

Railton, Peter (1986) 'Moral realism', *Philosophical Review* 95: 163–207.

Rappeport, Mike (2003) 'The democratic ethos and the positive sum society', *Society* 40(5): 36–43.

Rawls, John (1972) *A theory of justice*. Oxford: Oxford University Press.

Rawls, John (2001) *Justice as fairness: A restatement*. Erin Kelly, ed. Cambridge, Mass.: Harvard University Press.

Rechard, R. P. (1999) 'Historical relationship between performance assessment for radioactive waste disposal and other types of risk assessment', *Risk Analysis* 19(5): 763–807.

Reddy, Sanjay G. (1996) 'Claims to expert knowledge and the subversion of democracy: the triumph of risk over uncertainty', *Economy and Society* 25: 222–54.

Reibetanz, Sophia (1998) 'Contractualism and aggregation', *Ethics* 108: 296–311.

Ringer, Fritz K. (1989) 'Causal analysis in historical reasoning', *History and Theory* 28: 154–72.

Ringquist, E. J. (2000) 'Environmental justice: normative concerns and empirical evidence'. In N. J. Vig and M. E. Kraft, eds, *Environmental policy: New directions for the twenty-first century*. Washington, D.C.: CQ Press. 232–56.
Ripstein, Arthur (1994) 'Equality, luck, and responsibility', *Philosophy and Public Affairs* 23: 3–23.
Ripstein, Arthur (1999) *Equality, responsibility and the law*. Cambridge: Cambridge University Press.
Rizzi, Dominick A. and Stig Andur Pedersen (1992) 'Causality in medicine: towards a theory and terminology', *Theoretical Medicine* 13: 233–54.
Robespierre, Maximilien ([1794] 1967), 'Sur les principes de morale politique qui doivent guider la Convention nationale dans l'administration intérieure de la République'. In *Œuvres de Maximilien Robespierre*, Marc Bouloiseau and Albert Soboul, eds, Tome X. Paris: Presses Universitaires de France. 350–67.
Rogerson, Kenneth F. (1984) 'Rights at risk', *Southwest Philosophy Review* 1: 119–30.
Rosebury, Brian (1995) 'Moral responsibility and "moral luck"', *Philosophical Review* 104: 499–524.
Rosencrantz, Holger, Karin Edvardsson, and Sven Ove Hansson (2007) 'Vision zero – Is it irrational?', *Transportation Research Part A: Policy and Practice* 41: 559–67.
Ross, Alf (1941) 'Imperatives and logic', *Theoria* 7: 53–71.
Ross, Andrew and H. Damon Matthews (2009). 'Climate engineering and the risk of rapid climate change', *Environmental Research Letters* 4: 1–6.
Rothschild, Michael and Joseph E. Stiglitz (1970) 'Increasing risk: I. A definition', *Journal of Economic Theory* 2: 225–43.
Rothschild, Victor (1978), 'Risk – The Richard Dimbleby lecture', *The Listener*, 1978(30): 715–18.
Rousseau, Denis L. (1992). 'Case studies in pathological science', *American Scientist* 80(1): 54–63.
Royal Society (1983) *Risk assessment: Report of a Royal Society study group*. London: Royal Society.
Rudén, Christina and Sven Ove Hansson (2008) 'Evidence based toxicology – "sound science" in new guise', *International Journal of Occupational and Environmental Health* 14: 299–306.
Russell, Bertrand (1913) 'On the notion of a cause', *Proceedings of the Aristotelian Society* 13: 1–26. Reprinted in Bertrand Russell (1994) *Mysticism and logic*, London: Routledge. 173–99.
Russell, Bertrand (1966) *Philosophical essays*, rev. ed. (first edition 1910). London: Allen and Unwin.
Russo, J. Edward and Paul J. H. Schoemaker (1989) *Decision traps: the ten barriers to brilliant decision-making and how to overcome them*. New York: Doubleday.
Ruthen, Russell (1993) 'Strange matters', *Scientific American* 269(2): 17.
Sartorius R., ed. (1983) *Paternalism*. Minnesota: University of Minnesota Press.
Savage, Leonard J. (1972) *The foundations of statistics*, 2nd edition. New York: Dover.
Scanlon, Thomas M., (1998) *What we owe to each other*, Cambridge Mass.: Harvard University Press.
Schoemaker, Paul J. H. (1982) 'The expected utility model: its variants, purposes, evidence and limitations', *Journal of Economic Literature* 20: 529–63.

Schroeder, C. H. (1986) 'Rights against risks', *Columbia Law Review* 86: 495–562.
Segall, Shlomi (2010) *Health, luck and justice*. Princeton: Princeton University Press.
Sen, Amartya (1979) 'Utilitarianism and welfarism', *Journal of Philosophy* 76(9): 463–89.
Sen, Amartya (1983) 'Evaluator-relativity and consequential evaluation', *Philosophy and Public Affairs* 12: 113–32.
Sen, Amartya (1999) *Development as freedom*. New York: Alfred A. Knopf.
Sen, Amartya (2000) 'Consequential evaluation and practical reason', *Journal of Philosophy* 97: 477–502.
Shrader-Frechette, Kristin (1987) 'Parfit and mistakes in moral mathematics', *Ethics* 98: 50–60.
Shrader-Frechette, Kristin (1988) 'Parfit, risk assessment and imperceptible effects', *Public Affairs Quarterly* 2: 75–96.
Shrader-Frechette, Kristin (2002) *Environmental justice: Creating equality, reclaiming democracy*. New York: Oxford University Press.
Sidgwick, Henry ([1907] 1962) *The methods of ethics*, 7th ed. London: MacMillan.
Simmons, J. (1987) 'Consent and fairness in planning land use', *Business and Professional Ethics Journal* 6(2): 5–20.
Simons, Kenneth W. (1999) 'Negligence'. In Ellen Frankel Paul, Fred D. Miller, Jr., and Jeffrey Paul, eds, *Responsibility*. Cambridge: Cambridge University Press. 52–93.
Sin, Don D., Larry W. Svenson, Robert L. Cowie, and S. F. Paul Man (2003) 'Can universal access to health care eliminate health inequities between children of poor and nonpoor families?' *Chest* 124: 51–6.
Singer, Marcus (1977) 'Actual consequence utilitarianism', *Mind* 86: 67–77.
Singer, Marcus (1982) 'Incoherence, inconsistency, and moral theory: More on actual consequence utilitarianism', *Southern Journal of Philosophy* 20: 375–91.
Sinnott-Armstrong, Walter (1999) 'Some varieties of particularism', *Metaphilosophy* 30: 1–12.
Skorupski, John (1995) 'Agent-neutrality, consequentialism, utilitarianism ... a terminological note', *Utilitas* 7: 49–54.
Slote, Michael (1984) 'Satisficing consequentialism', *Aristotelian Society, Supplementary Volume* 58: 139–64.
Smart, J. J. C. and Bernard Williams (1973) *Utilitarianism for and against*. London: Cambridge University Press.
Sobel, David (2012) 'Backing away from libertarian self-ownership', *Ethics* 123: 32–60.
Sosa, David (1993) 'Consequences of consequentialism', *Mind* 102: 101–22.
Spielthenner, Georg (2005) 'Consequentialism or deontology?', *Philosophia* 33: 217–35.
Spohn, W. (1977) 'Where Luce and Krantz do really generalize Savage's decision model', *Erkenntnis* 11, 113–34.
Spurgin, Earl W. (2006) 'Occupational safety and paternalism: Machan revisited', *Journal of Business Ethics* 63: 155–73.
Stark, Cynthia (2000) 'Hypothetical consent and justification', *Journal of Philosophy* 97: 313–34.
Steigleder, Klaus (2013) 'Risk and rights: towards a rights-based risk ethics', manuscript.

Strasser, Mark (1989) 'Actual versus probable utilitarianism', *Southern Journal of Philosophy* 27: 585–97.
Sugden, Robert (1985) Regret, recrimination and rationality, *Theory and Decision* 19: 77–99.
Sugden, Robert (2003) 'Opportunity as a space for individuality: its value and the impossibility of measuring it', *Ethics* 113: 783–809.
Taylor, P. (1984) *Smoke ring: The politics of tobacco*. London: Bodley Head.
Teuber, Andreas (1990), 'Justifying risk', *Daedalus* 119: 235–54.
Thomson, Judith J. (1984) 'Remarks on causation and liability', *Philosophy and Public Affairs* 13: 101–33.
Thomson, Judith J. (1986) *Rights, restitution and risk: Essays in moral theory*. Cambridge Mass.: Harvard University Press.
Thomson, Judith J. (1990) *The realm of rights*. Cambridge Mass.: Harvard University Press.
Trachtman, Leon E. (1985) 'Why tolerate the statistical victim?', *Hastings Center Report* 15(1): 14.
Trebilcot, Joyce (1974) 'Aprudentialism', *American Philosophical Quarterly* 11: 203–10.
Urmson, J. O. (1958) 'Saints and heroes'. In A. I. Melden, ed., *Essays in moral philosophy*. Seattle: University of Washington Press. 198–216.
Vainio, Harri and Lorenzo Tomatis (1985) 'Exposure to carcinogens: scientific and regulatory aspects', *Annals of the American Conference of Governmental Industrial Hygienists* 12: 135–143.
Vallentyne, Peter (1987) 'Utilitarianism and the outcome of actions', *Pacific Philosophical Quarterly* 68: 57–70.
Van de Vate, Dwight and James Kelly (1978) 'The concept of risk', *Southern Journal of Philosophy* 16: 115–23.
van Hees, Martin (2004) 'Freedom of choice and diversity of options: Some difficulties', *Social Choice and Welfare* 22: 253–66.
Vanden Houten, Art (2002) 'Prudence in Hobbes's political philosophy', *History of Political Thought* 23: 266–87.
Viscusi, W. Kip (2002) 'The new cigarette paternalism', *Regulation* 25(4): 58–64.
von Wright, Georg Henrik (1951) 'Deontic logic', *Mind* 60: 1–15.
von Wright, Georg Henrik (1963) *The varieties of goodness*. London: Routledge & Kegan Paul.
von Wright, Georg Henrik (1968) *An essay in deontic logic and the general theory of action, Acta Philosophica Fennica* 21.
Waddington, C. H. (1960) *The ethical animal*. London: George Allen & Unwin.
Walzer, Michael (1983) *Spheres of justice*. New York: Basic Books.
Ward, David E. (1995) 'Imaginary scenarios, black boxes and philosophical method', *Erkenntnis* 43: 181–98.
Wattles, Jeffrey (1996) *The golden rule*. New York: Oxford University Press.
Weale, Alfred (1979) 'Statistical lives and the principle of maximum benefit', *Journal of Medical Ethics* 5: 185–95.
Weber, M. (1998) 'The resilience of the Allais paradox', *Ethics* 109: 94–118.
Weijer, Charles, Stanley H. Shapiro, and Kathleen Cranley Glass (2000) 'Clinical equipoise and not the uncertainty principle is the moral underpinning of the randomised controlled trial', *British Medical Journal* 321: 756–57.

Weirich, Paul (1981) 'A bias of rationality', *Australasian Journal of Philosophy* 59: 31–7.

Wellman, Carl (1975) 'Upholding legal rights', *Ethics* 86: 49–60.

Whiting, Jennifer (2006) 'The Nicomachean account of philia'. In Richard Kraut (ed.) *The Blackwell guide to Aristotle's Nicomachean Ethics*. Oxford: Blackwell. 276–304.

Wilkinson, Richard and Kate Pickett (2009) *The spirit level*. London: Allen Lane.

Williams, Bernard (1973) 'Ethical consistency'. In *Problems of the self: Philosophical essays 1956–1972*. London: Cambridge University Press. 166–186.

Williams, Bernard (1976) 'Moral luck', *Aristotelian Society, Supplementary Volume* 50: 115–35.

Williams, Bernard (1981) *Moral luck: Philosophical papers 1973–1980*. Cambridge: Cambridge University Press.

Wilson, Robert A. (1971) 'Anomie in the ghetto: A study of neighborhood type, race, and anomie', *American Journal of Sociology* 77: 66–88.

Wit, Ernst-Jan (1997) *The ethics of chance*. Ph.D. Thesis, Pennsylvania State University.

Wynne, Brian (1992) 'Carving out science (and politics) in the regulatory jungle', *Social Studies of Science* 22: 745–58.

Zamir, Tzachi (2001) 'One consequence of consequentialism: morality and over-determination', *Erkenntnis* 55: 155–68.

Zazryn, Tsharni R., Paul R. McCrory, and Peter A. Cameron (2008) 'Neurologic injuries in boxing and other combat sports', *Neurologic Clinics* 26: 257–70.

Zeelenberg, M., J. Beattie, J. van der Pligt and N. K. de Vries (1996) 'Consequences of regret aversion: Effects of expected feedback on risky decision making', *Organizational Behavior and Human Decision Processes* 65: 148–58.

Zeelenberg, Marcel (1999) 'Anticipated regret, expected feedback and behavioral decision making', *Journal of Behavioural Decision Making* 12: 93–106.

Zeelenberg, Marcel and Rik Pieters (2004) 'Consequences of regret aversion in real life: The case of the Dutch postcode lottery', *Organizational Behavior and Human Decision Processes* 93: 155–68.

Zeelenberg, Marcel and Rik Pieters (2007) 'A theory of regret regulation 1.0', *Journal of Consumer Psychology* 17: 3–18.

Zimmerman, M. J. (2006) 'Risk, rights, and restitution', *Philosophical Studies* 128: 285–311.

Zimmerman, M. J. (2008) *Living with uncertainty: The moral significance of ignorance*. Cambridge, UK: Cambridge University Press.

Index

absolutism, probabilistic, 29, 35, 132
accelerator, 92
acceptable risk, 97
acceptance, 120
accident investigation, 138
ACGIH, 113–14
action-guidance, 25–7, 130
  decision guidance, 66, 75
actualism, 24–7, 42, 130
addiction, 122–3
  see also smoking
additivity, 9
afterthought, 72
  see also hypothetical retrospection
agency, 44–6, 48–9, 57
alternative
  cause, 91–2
  effect, 141
  option, 136
analogue, closest deterministic, 50–1, 134
antipaternalism, extended, 122–5
appraisal, moral, 22, 127
Aquinas, Thomas, 61, 136
Archimedean point, 133
Aristotle, 144
Arnauld, Antoine, 128
astronomy, 52
asymmetry
  epistemic, 66
  in error tendencies, 80
autonomy, 117

baby lottery, 142
Bayesianism, 14
benefit, 30, 36, 43
Bentham, Jeremy, 46
Bernoulli, Daniel, 128
betting, 11, 65
bias, 80, 116
binary relation, 128
biotechnology, 14, 88, 109
boxing, 123–5
Boyle, Robert, 53, 135
branches, future, 63, 65–6, 70–3, 136–7

calibration, of probability, 129
cancelling, 99–100, 141
care, due, 98
Cartesius (Descartes), 53
catastrophe, large, 26, 78–9, 88–9, 92, 110, 129
causality, 8, 22, 44, 46–7, 51–4, 66, 71, 121–4, 130, 134–5
  alternative cause, 91–2
  causal chain, 53, 55, 135
  causal field, 135
  causal tree, 55–6
  mental, 46
  transitivity, 53–4
cautiousness, 28, 140
  risk aversion, 28, 40, 131
certainty, 12
chain, causal, 53, 55, 135
chance
  equal opportunity, 106–7, 133, 142
  randomness, 54–5, 84, 112–13, 138, 142
change in preference, 137
chemicals, persistent, 92
children, 77, 105–7, 115–16
classes, social, 104–5
climate change, 14, 82, 92, 125, 140
climatology, 53
clinical trials, 84–8, 120
clockwork universe, 53
  determinism, 1–2, 53–4, 63, 107, 127
code, moral, 31
cognitive limitations, 14
commitment, 33–4, 37
comparability, 15, 141
comparison, 8, 67–8, 127–8, 137
compensability, 141
complex systems, 92

compromise, 109
concerning, 131
conflict, moral, 34
conflict avoidance, 34
conflict evadability, 33–4, 37
conflict-free specification, 31–3, 37
Confucius, 62
consensus, 39, 108–10
consent, 10, 38, 43, 116–21, 131–2, 143–5
  actual, 38
  hypothetical, 39, 133
  informed, 84, 117, 120
consequence, 23, 42, 44, 47, 56, 88, 133, 135
  actual, 24–5
  analytical, 134
  broad, 47, 49
  combined, 47, 56
  conceptual, 134
  counterfactual, 24–5
  direct, 46–7, 134
  effaced, 45
  non-causal, 134
  random, 54
  total, 54–6, 135
consequentialism, 23–4, 45, 47–50, 135
  broad, 47, 49
consumer products, 116
contract theory (contractualism), 37–41, 43, 62, 132–3
control, 17–20, 65, 107–8
  illusion of, 13
  uncertainty about, 19
cost, sunk, 129
cost-benefit analysis (risk-benefit analysis), 23, 26, 98, 127, 130
Cottingham, John, 116
counterfactual consequence, 24–5
crime, 117–19, 144

de minimis, 97
decision framing, 15, 41, 78
decision guidance, 66, 75
  action guidance, 25–7, 130
decision matrice, 17
decision rule
  expected utility, 9–10, 24, 26–8, 41–2, 74–80, 128, 130, 138
  maximin, 40–3, 70, 74, 131, 133
  minimax regret, 131
decision stability, 64, 69, 138
decision theory, 1, 2, 15, 17, 44, 51, 55, 67, 76, 132, 134
  Bayesian, 14
defeasance problem, 100–2, 109
defeasibility, 28–9, 35, 97–100
demarcation of decision, 15, 41, 78
democracy, 104, 109–10, 120, 125–6, 143
deontic logic, 134
deontology (duty-based ethics), 21, 28–34, 43, 45, 131
desalination, 90
Descartes, René, 53
description-dependence, 134
determinism, 1–2, 53–4, 63, 107, 127
deterministic analogue, 50–3, 134
detriment, 128
Dickenson, Donna, 137
dilemma, moral, 33, 70, 139
disambiguation, 89
disaster, large, 26, 78–9, 88–9, 92, 110, 129
discourse ethics, 129
dissonance reduction, 67
division of labour, 102
drug addiction, 122–3
  see also smoking
duelling, 124
duty
  definition, 131
  see also obligation
duty-based (deontology), 21, 28–34, 43, 45, 131

economic system, 92
economics, 53
ecosystem, 92
effect, 45, 134
  alternative, 141
  causal, 46
  imperceptible, 143
  opposite, 90–1
  undetectable, 111–16, 143
  see also consequence
egoism, 61, 136
Ellsberg, Daniel, 140

empathy, 62
end state, 45, 65
epidemiology, 113, 115
EPR paradox, 53
equality
  between genders, 133
  see justice
equipoise, 84, 88, 140
error, 80, 138
ethics (moral philosophy), 1–2, 17, 21, 53, 56, 62, 123, 125–7
ethos, democratic, 109–10
evolution, 131
examples
  addictive soft drink, 123
  anti-bribery rule, 31
  artificial photosynthesis, 90
  bacteria causing leukocytes causing healing, 53
  beating a cat, 31
  bequeathing to animal society, 34
  betting on horse, 65
  blaming patient for failure, 19
  borrowing lawn-mower, 35, 131
  breaking antique vase, 45–6
  broken shutter release button, 52
  bungee jump, 118–19
  buying gym membership, 19
  car-driving, 22, 29, 36, 100–3
  cause of cholera, 52
  choice of cleaning agent, 82–3
  choice of pharmaceutical, 83
  choice of university position, 66
  choice of vacation trip, 50, 70, 75
  dangerous work, 9, 98, 118
  decision to return early from pub, 65
  deep-sea divers, 9
  dinner invitation, 47
  discharging industrial waste, 91
  divorce, 20
  driving drunk, 25
  driving passengers without seatbelts, 123
  execution of Louis XVI, 55
  explosions in building, 7, 16, 80
  faulty bolt in roller-coaster, 44–5
  fire alarm system, 67–8
  fire in Kuala Lumpur, 47
  flipping coin about cleaning task, 79
  flushing thinner into toilet, 56
  food additive, 30
  gas leakage, 27, 52
  genetically altered earthworm, 14
  geoengineering, 14
  give dog to a child, 24–5
  imposter receiving silver object, 100
  insolvent with two creditors, 37
  investment decisions, 64, 77, 88, 119–20
  killing in self-defence, 64
  landmines, 11
  lawn-crossing, 135
  lending lawn-mower, 35, 131
  meeting king in sanctuary, 31–2
  microalgae for chemical synthesis, 90
  nano divide, 91–2
  new steering device, 76–7
  nuclear waste, 15
  overloading a bridge, 25
  paying for better mark, 15
  pistol believed to be empty, 88, 92–3
  prime minister risking defection, 11
  punch press vs. motorcar, 124–5
  puncture someone's bicycle tyres, 34
  regicide, 55, 134
  risky but life-saving surgery, 41
  risky mine, 118
  Russian roulette on sleeping person, 49–50
  saving acquaintance or random victim, 138
  saving ice-cream for tomorrow, 62
  seaside trip with uncertain weather, 75
  seat belts, 76
  self-defence, 64
  serving unhealthy food, 29
  seven dies Russian roulette, 98
  short-cut through dark park, 117–19
  smoking cessation, 18, 89–90
  smoking for just three weeks, 18
  society with two classes, 104–5

stopping at red lights, 32
suing ex-husband, 63
surgery, 41
taking single chocolate piece, 65
therapeutic microorganism becomes virulent, 13
three carcinogenic substances, 112–15
throwing down brick on person, 48–9
tickets to Wagner or Verdi, 81
transmitting a cold, 29
transportation of nuclear material, 9
trustee making risky investments, 77
two meetings at same time, 33
vaccination, 30
world's highest building, 16
exception clause, 32, 99
excuses, moral, 111–26
existential risks, 78–9, 88–9, 92, 110, 129
expectable value, 130
expectation value, 9–10, 87, 140
see also expected utility
expected utility, 9–10, 24, 26–8, 41–2, 74–80, 128, 130, 138
experts, 13, 110, 113, 119, 129
exploitation, 102–3, 145
exposure limits, 114
extended antipaternalism, 122–5

fair risk exchange, 108
fairness (justice), 10, 27–8, 61, 77, 80, 91, 104–8, 138, 142
fallacy
sheer size, 141
tuxedo, 13
feedback, 137
Feinberg, Joel, 145
foresight argument, 62–5
framing of decision, 15, 41, 78
Frankena, W.K. 32
frequency, 129
friendship, 144
Fröding, Barbro viii, 144
fundamentalism, 126
fusion energy, 92

gambling metaphor, 13, 129
game theory, 16–18, 133
Gauthier, David, 133
gender equality, 133
generation, 105
genetic technology, 14, 88, 109
golden rule, 62
Goldman, Alan, 99
gravitation, 52
great uncertainty, 14–17, 88–93, 139
greenhouse effect (climate change), 14, 82, 92, 125, 140
guilt, 64

Hare, R.M. 132–3
harm, 129–130
Harsanyi, J.C. 41, 133
hazard, 127
health insurance, 106
Health Physics Society, 114, 143–4
Helsinki declaration, 144
Hobbes, Thomas, 38, 61, 132, 136
holocaust, 125
Huguenot movement, 132
hypothetical retrospection, 64–73, 84, 86, 136–7, 139
hypothetical uncertainty, 40

ideal decision situation, 39
ideal observer, 62, 132
idealization, 2, 13, 44, 51–2, 127
identity, of persons, 63, 112, 116
impartiality, 116
imperceptible risk, 143
indetectable risk, 111–16, 143
index, of cautiousness, 140
individuality, 107
influence, 104, 108, 119–20
maximal equal, 108
information, loss of, 66
initial situation (original position), 39–43, 133, 136
intention, 10, 36, 48–9, 57
intentional threats, 16
International Organization for Standardization, 128
intuitions, moral, 61, 72–3
IPCC, 82, 140

Jeffrey, Richard, 137

Jesus, 62
justice (fairness), 10, 27–8, 61, 77, 80, 91, 104–8, 138, 142

Kant, Immanuel, 28, 133
Keynes, J.M. 129
Knight, Frank, 129
knowledge, lack of, 7

labour, division of, 102
latency period, 144
law of large numbers, 77–8, 80
law of nature, 54
leeway, moral, 80–3, 88
Leibniz, Gottfried Wilhelm, 127
levelling-out effect, 78–9
libertarianism, 34
life-style risk, 121
lightning, 128
Lima Rego, Margarida, 128
lives, statistical, 112

majority, 39, 132
malevolent action, 16
Marcus, Ruth Barcan, 33–4
maximal equal influence, 108
maximin rule, 40–3, 70, 74, 131, 133
McCarthy, David, 116
mechanical universe, 53
medical ethics, 84–8, 117, 120, 125, 140, 144
mental state, 48
metadecision, 78
Mill, John Stuart, 52, 122–3
miners, trapped, 112, 116
minimax regret, 131
minority, 110, 143
mixture appraisal problem, 22–4, 29, 34–5, 37–40, 42, 50–1
Mo Tzu (Mozi), 62
Mohammed, 62
Möller, Niklas, viii
monarchy, 132
Moore, George Edward, 130
moral appraisal, 22, 127
moral code, 31
moral dilemma, 33, 70, 139
moral philosophy, 1–2, 17, 21, 53, 56, 62, 123, 125–7
moral theory, 21, 43–4, 51, 56, 125–7, 130, 132
motive, 46, 48

Nagel, Thomas, 137
nanotechnology, 14, 88, 91
National Research Council, 128
natural rights, 43
natural risk, 141
natural state, 38
neutrality
  temporal, 137
  towards risk, 80, 139
Newton, Isaac, 53
Nicole, Pierre, 128
no harm principle, 99
norms, 22
Norns, 79
novelty, 92
Nozick, Robert, 35–6, 106
nuclear energy, 9, 15, 92, 109, 139
nuclear war, 78–9, 125, 129
nullify, 141

obeyability, 131
objectivity, 10–12, 128
obligation (duty), 28, 48, 66, 131
  assessment, 31
  conflicting, 29, 31, 33, 70, 139
  correlative, 34
  residual, 141
  rule of, 31
  special, 115–16
  veritable, 131
observer, ideal, 62, 132
occupational risks, 9, 98, 113–19, 121, 123–5, 144
opportunity
  equal, 106–7, 133, 142
  set, 50
opposite effect, 90–1
optimism, 40, 140
optimism-pessimism index, 140
original position (initial situation), 39–43, 133, 136
outcome, 9, 45
  of treatment, 85
  see also consequence
overriding, 99–100

owner, single, 98

package (of risks and benefits), 117–19
paralysis, problem of, 131
Parfit, Derek, 63, 143
Part Royal Logic, 128
partiality, 116
participation, 119
  influence, 104, 108, 119–20
particle accelerator, 92
paternalism, 117, 122, 125, 145
payment, 117
Pentagon, 79
permission
  categorical, 34
  grantable, 34
  revocable, 132
persistent chemicals, 92
perspective
  personal, 62–3
  temporal, 62–73
pessimism, 40, 140
pesticide, 92, 103
photosynthesis, artificial, 90
physics, 53
plan, 137
Plato, 136
polywater, 88–9
population dynamics, 53
possibility, 16
  mere, 88–93
  unknown, 15
  valuation of, 92
practice, social, 142
prediction, 138
preference change, 137
prima facie, 35, 99
Prior, A.N. 135
prioritarianism, 28
probability, 8, 11, 15, 18, 23, 29, 55, 127–8
  absolutism, 29, 35, 132
  estimate of, 13, 16–17, 20, 74–5, 80, 83, 85, 140
  limit to, 30, 36, 97, 132
  reduction to, 14
  sensitivity to, 41
  uncertainty about, 13, 79, 83–8
process orientation, 45, 50
prohibition, 28
property, of action, 23
prudence, 61, 136

quantification, 8–10, 127–8
quantum entanglement, 53

radiation, 113–14, 143
randomization, 84, 86
randomness (chance), 54–5, 84, 112–13, 138, 142
Rasmussen report, 9
ratifiability, 137
Rawls, John, 38–41, 43, 133, 136–7
real estate prices, 144
realism, moral, 145
reasoning
  interpersonal, 62–3
  intertemporal, 62–73
recusal, 116
refutationism, 73
regret, 64, 67, 69, 131, 137–8
  minimax, 131
remorse, 137
residue, moral (residual obligation), 100, 141
responsibility, 123–4, 133
result, 134
  see also consequence
retrospection, hypothetical, 64–73, 84, 86, 136–7, 139
right, moral term, 25
rights, 45, 48, 66, 97, 99, 131–2, 144
  absolute, 37
  correlative, 34, 37
  defeasible, 35
  natural, 34
rights-based ethics, 34–7, 43, 100
risk
  acceptable, 97
  additivity of, 9
  aversion to, 28, 40, 131
  comparison, 8, 127–8
  definition, 7–12
  double nature, 11
  drift in sense, 10
  exchanges of, 101–10, 142

existential, 78–9, 88–9, 92, 110, 129
imperceptible, 143
imposition, 3, 28, 30, 48–50, 56–7, 61, 97–8, 104, 111, 114–17, 119, 129, 132
indetectable, 111–16, 143
life-style, 121
natural, 141
neutrality, 80, 139
new, 92
objective, 10–12
occupational, 9, 98, 113–19, 121, 123–5, 144
quantification, 8–10, 127–8
reciprocal, 101–10, 142
self-inflicted, 119, 121–5, 145
subjective, 10–12
taking, 45, 51, 57, 67, 138
"under risk," 11, 13
undetectable, 111–16, 143
value-laden, 10–11
victim's contribution, 121–5
risk analysis, 23, 49, 104, 109, 128, 131, 138, 141
probabilistic, 26, 48, 50, 130
risk-benefit analysis (cost-benefit analysis), 23, 26, 98, 127, 130
Robespierre, Maximilien, 109–10, 143
Ross, Alf, 134
Ross, W.D., 28–9
roulette, 13
Russian, 49–50, 98
Royal Society, 128
rule
abidance, 49
golden, 62
maximin, 40–3, 70, 74, 131, 133
minimax regret, 131
of obligation, 31
Russell, Bertrand, 52–3, 130
Russian roulette, 49–50, 98

sabotage, 16
safety, 16
sanitation, 91
satisficing, 139
seat belts, 139
security, 16
security level, 40, 70, 87
self-defence, 99
self-determination, 117
self-harm, 119, 121–5, 145
self-mastery, 19
Sen, Amartya, 23, 46, 134
sensitivity, 128
sheer size fallacy, 141
Shrader-Frechette, Kristin, 143
Sidgwick, Henry, 67, 136
Singer, Marcus, 24
single owner, 98
slavery, voluntary, 145
Smart, J.J.C. 130
smoking, 112, 121–4
social contract, 37–41, 43, 62, 132–3
Socrates, 136
Sosa, David, 46, 48
spatio-temporal limits, 92
speed limit, 125
stability
of decisions, 64, 69, 138
notion, 141
starting line, 106–7, 142
state
mental, 48
of nature, 38
statistical victim, 112, 116
Steigleder, Klaus, viii
Stone, Robert, 113
strangers, 116, 144
subjective risk, 10–12
suicide, 123
sum-ranking, 23–4
sunk cost, 129
supererogation, 139
superstition, 89
symmetry
epistemic, 66
error tendencies, 80
tests, 90–2

temporal perspectives, 64–73
terrorism, 16–17, 125, 143
test
alternative causes, 91–2
alternative effects, 141
opposite effects, 90–1
symmetry, 90–2
Thomson, Judith, 117

threshold limit value, 114
thunder, 128
Thünen, J.H. von, 129
tort liability, 142
transduction, 81–4
transitivity, 53–4, 135
tree, causal, 55–6
  see also branches, future
trolley problem, 1
trust, 120
tuxedo fallacy, 13

uncertainty
  about control, 19
  about demarcation, 15
  about probabilities, 13, 79, 83–8
  about values, 127, 130
  definition, 11–17, 129
  great, 14–17, 88–93, 139
  hypothetical, 40
  moral effects, 80–8
  principle of, 140
  transduction, 81–4
  "under uncertainty," 13
uncontroversial values, 11
undetectable risk, 111–16, 143
unit risk factor, 9
United States, 105–6
utilitarianism, 21, 23–8, 30, 36, 42, 57, 66, 126, 130, 135, 141

Vallentyne, Peter viii, 131
valuation of possibilities, 92
value-carrier, 22
values, uncontroversial, 11
veil of ignorance, 40
veto, 39, 57, 108, 143
victim
  blaming, 124
  contributing to risk, 121–5
  identified, 116
  random, 138
  statistical, 116
viewpoint, 136
vinyl chloride, 114
virtue ethics, 22, 129
voluntariness, 10, 48–9, 57, 106, 117, 144
  see also consent

Walzer, Michael, 142
Weirich, Paul, viii
welfare, 142
welfarism, 23–4
Williams, Bernard, 141
Wit, Ernst-Jan, 137
workplace risks, 9, 98, 113–19, 121, 123–5, 144
worst cases, 41
wrong, moral term, 25

GPSR Compliance
The European Union's (EU) General Product Safety Regulation (GPSR) is a set of rules that requires consumer products to be safe and our obligations to ensure this.

If you have any concerns about our products, you can contact us on

ProductSafety@springernature.com

In case Publisher is established outside the EU, the EU authorized representative is:

Springer Nature Customer Service Center GmbH
Europaplatz 3
69115 Heidelberg, Germany

www.ingramcontent.com/pod-product-compliance
Ingram Content Group UK Ltd.
Pitfield, Milton Keynes, MK11 3LW, UK
UKHW020155290926
15471UKWH00005B/878

* 9 7 8 1 3 4 9 4 6 2 3 1 5 *